LEGENDS
OF
ATLANTIS
AND
LOST LEMURIA

Cover Art by Brian Asimor

LEGENDS
OF
ATLANTIS
AND
LOST LEMURIA

W. Scott-Elliot

This publication is made possible with the assistance of the Kern Foundation

The Theosophical Publishing House

Wheaton, IL U.S.A./Madras, India/London, England

THE STORY OF ATLANTIS first printed 1896
THE LOST LEMURIA first printed 1904
First combined edition published 1925
under the title THE STORY OF ATLANTIS
AND THE LOST LEMURIA by
The Theosophical Publishing House, Ltd., London.

A publication of the Theosophical Publishing House,
a department of the Theosophical Society in America.

Library of Congress Cataloging-in-Publication Data

Scott-Elliot, W.
   [Story of Atlantis]
   Legends of Atlantis; and, Lost Lemuria / W. Scott-Elliot.
      p.   cm.
   Reprint, with a new introd. Originally published: The story of
Atlantis, and The Lost Lemuria. London : Theosophical Pub. House,
1972.
   ISBN 0-8356-0664-3 : $12.95
   1. Atlantis.   2. Lemuria.   I. Scott-Elliot, W. Lost Lemuria.
1990. II. Title. III. Title: Legends of Atlantis.
GN751.S43   1990
398′.42—dc20   90-50203
                                                              CIP

Printed in the United States of America

Contents

About the Authors

W. Scott-Elliot is one of the classic authors of the Theosophical tradition. An early member of the London Lodge of the Theosophical Society, in 1899 he was awarded the T. Subba Row Medal for outstanding literary work in esoteric science and philosophy.

Charles Webster Leadbeater, on whose research the book is partly based, has been called the "Master-Scientist of Occultism." A member of the London Lodge at the same time as Scott-Elliot, he shared with the latter the results of his investigations into the inner planes, which included access to maps and records dealing with the lost continents of Atlantis and Lemuria.

John Algeo, who wrote the new preface, is Professor of English at the University of Georgia. A specialist in linguistics, he serves as consultant for a variety of organizations such as the National Endowment for the Humanities.

Publisher's Preface

W. Scott-Elliot's *The Story of Atlantis* and his *The Lost Lemuria* are being republished as historical documents that add to our knowledge of the ever-present myths of these sunken lands which are alleged to be so important in the history of the human race. This new edition includes a preface by John Algeo, a professor of English and a linguist, that sets the pieces in the context of the ongoing speculation and research into these myths.

The Story of Atlantis first came out in 1896 and *The Lost Lemuria* in 1904. There have been new editions and reprints of each, and an edition combining both came out first in 1925 and has been slightly revised and reprinted several times since. This new edition reproduces the 1914 version of *Atlantis* and the original 1904 version of *Lemuria,* unedited except that marginal headings have been run into the text and the pages numbered sequentially.

Transactions of the Blavatsky Lodge referred to in the text is a volume of the proceedings of the London Lodge where H. P. Blavatsky was active for a time. It was first published in 1890 by the Theosophical Press, London, and is still available through Theosophical libraries and book stores.

Preface to the 1990 Edition
Atlantis and Lemuria: Myth and History
JOHN ALGEO

Atlantis and Lemuria are two fabled lost continents, one in the Atlantic and the other in the Indian Ocean. Interest in them, however, is of very different antiquity. Stories about Atlantis go back to Plato, who lived in the fourth and fifth centuries before Christ. The existence of Lemuria, on the other hand, was not hypothesized until the middle of the nineteenth century. The story of Atlantis was first told by philosophers and poets; Lemuria began as a scientific hypothesis.

It was inevitable, however, that the two lost continents should be related to each other. W. Scott-Elliot (W. Williamson) was not the first to deal with the two lands in a single framework, but his accounts—originally published as separate books (in 1896 and 1904) and then combined as the two parts of one volume, as here—are the most accessible and coherent descriptions of the lost continents from the standpoint of the esoteric tradition.

Lemuria is a relative late-comer to the gazetteer of lost continents, but Atlantis is one of the most enduring myths of the Western world. Like all good myths, it is part history and part metaphor, in this case combining two great universal motifs—that of the flood and that of paradise lost. The interest that the story of Atlantis has evoked during the past 2500 years is an indication of the power of that story over the human imagination.

Origins of the Myth

The legend of Atlantis that is the basis of all later versions derives from two of Plato's dialogs, the *Timaeus* and the *Critias.* The *Timaeus* follows and summarizes another dialog, the *Republic,* in which Socrates talks about the ideal state, the perfect utopia. One of the participants in the dialog, Critias, offers to tell a story that has come down in his family since the days of the great lawgiver, Solon, who learned it from the priests of Egypt. The story concerns a war fought in primeval times between Athens—which in those days was very much the sort of ideal state that Socrates described—and a mighty sea-power called Atlantis. First, however, Timaeus speaks at length about the origin of the universe, and his account occupies the rest of the dialog named after him.

In the *Critias,* after Timaeus has finished speaking, Critias continues the story he promised to tell. The island continent of Atlantis, located beyond the Pillars of Hercules (the Strait of Gibraltar), was settled by ten sons of the god of the sea, Poseidon, the eldest and chief of whom was Atlas, after whom the country was named. Atlantis was a rich, productive, and peaceful land, ruled over by a divine dynasty. Its royal palace was on a circular island, surrounded by two larger ring-shaped islands, which were separated from each other and the mainland by three ring-shaped bodies of water—so that the plan of the city resembled a five-ringed target with the palace and temple of Poseidon at the center.

In time, however, the people of Atlantis deteriorated from a law-abiding, peaceful nation to a greedy, ambitious and warlike one. They set out to conquer Europe and Asia, but were opposed and defeated by the valorous primeval Athenians. After the military defeat of Atlantis, great earthquakes and floods swept the world and caused the island of Atlantis to sink beneath the ocean during a single day. These events took place about 11,500 years ago.

That, in broad outline, is the story told by Plato, and it is the origin of the Atlantis myth. All later versions are elaborations or adaptations of this account. As one commentator has observed, before Plato there is silence; after Plato, echoes.

The Meaning of the Myth

Plato's students disagreed about how to interpret his story of Atlantis, and from their day to our own that disagreement has continued. Briefly, there have been four main views of the story: historical, allegorical, parabolical, and mythical.

History: The most literal view is that Plato was recording actual history and that the facts are much as he gave them. The discovery of an underwater ridge in the Atlantic Ocean, which surfaces at the Azores and elsewhere, was taken for a while as evidence for the earlier existence of a continent. But that ridge, we now believe, has been gradually built up from the ocean floor as matter from within the planet is forced out. The ridge is not the remains of a former continent, but evidence of fissures in the earth that cause the spread of continental land masses. The story of Atlantis, as Plato told it, is not reconcilable with present-day scientific knowledge about the Atlantic Ocean.

A recent view of Atlantis as history is that Plato was actually talking about the civilization of Minoan Crete, which about 900 years before his time was destroyed by a volcanic eruption on the island of Thera (also called Santorini) and by consequent tidal waves. This theory holds that memories of the great Minoan maritime culture and its violent demise survived in oral legends to Plato's day, but that directions and times were confused. So Plato mistakenly located the land beyond the Pillars of Hercules in the Atlantic Ocean and got the time of its destruction wrong by a factor of ten, reporting it as 9000 years before his time. When it was first advanced, the Minoan theory was the object of a good deal of excited interest. But there are so many problems with the theory that many scholars no longer think it is probable, at least as the principal explanation of Plato's story.

Other historical interpretations have been made—linking Atlantis with Bimini, Scandinavia, and various other presently existing places in Europe, Africa, Asia, and the Americas. None of them is convincing.

There is probably some historical basis to Plato's story, as there is to the Trojan War as recorded by the Homeric epics, but a literal reading of Plato's dialog as historical fact is too simple and cannot be sustained.

Allegory: An alternative interpretation of Plato's story is that he only pretended to be recounting literal history—he was actually creating an allegory about the political realities and ideals of his own time. According to this interpretation, Plato's description of ancient Athens was actually an idealized portrait of how he thought a good society should be organized and function. His description of Atlantis, on the other hand, was a disguised representation of Athens in his own day, with the dangers that he foresaw threatening his city. In this interpretation, the war between Athens and Atlantis is simply that struggle between the ideal and the actual, and the physical destruction of Atlantis by submersion represents the political destruction of Athens that Plato feared.

It was dangerous, even in the cradle of democracy, as we think of Athens, to criticize the state. Socrates was condemned to death as a disturber of the social order. So if Plato wanted to point out to his fellow citizens the weaknesses of their society, allegory was safer than direct statement. Thus, this theory holds, Plato protected himself by presenting his views of a good, but imaginary government as the way Athens was in the distant past, and expressed his fears about the future of Athens by describing the destruction of an imaginary ancient land in the Atlantic Ocean.

A variant interpretation suggests that by Atlantis

Plato was allegorizing the land of Sicily, whose ruler Plato hoped would become a philosopher-king. However, the ruler was a disappointment and the land seemed to be degenerating, headed for destruction. So Plato wrote a warning under the allegory of Atlantis.

Parable: Another interpretation holds that rather than an allegory about a particular problem, the story of Atlantis is a tale with a general moral. Plato's dialogs contain a number of stories in whose literal truth he surely did not believe. These stories are fictions—but philosophical fictions or parables. That is, they are imaginative accounts he invented to express important truths about human nature and the world. For example, Plato describes a race of people who live in a cave and see nothing except shadows cast upon the wall by light whose source they never look upon. He also says that humans were once round, with four arms and legs, but later each was divided into two, and ever since each half has been searching for its matching side to unite with.

Plato did not believe in the literal truth of such stories, any more than Jesus believed in the literal truth of his stories about the prodigal son or the careless bridesmaids. Such stories are parables that express important psychological truths rather than historical events. The story of the cave says that we do not see reality directly, but only its shadowy images through our senses. The story of the divided humanity says that we do not exist separately, but as parts of an original unity, to which we long to return. Plato called such stories "useful lies" or "noble fictions.'' That is, they are literally false, but spiritually true.

As a "noble fiction," the story of Atlantis is about the benefits of cooperation and law-abidingness and the penalties of greed and ambition. It is a cautionary tale about how easy it is to degenerate from justice and happiness to violence and destruction.

Myth: A myth is different from any of the preceding, although it may combine various of their qualities. A myth may be founded upon historical fact, but its importance is far greater than a historical record. Jesus was a historical reality—a Jewish rabbi some two thousand years ago who taught and did marvelous things. Today we remember him, however, not for his historical reality as a popular preacher of the Jewish Law, but because he was transfigured in the minds and hearts of his later followers into a dying and resurrected God. He became a myth—and myths are far grander and more powerful than history.

Whether there really was a historical Atlantis of the kind Plato described or not, whether Plato intended a political allegory to instruct his fellow citizens or not, whether he was creating a philosophical parable or not, the story of Atlantis which he told has become a myth. There was doubtless some historical basis to the story, there certainly were allegorical parallels to Atlantis in Plato's world, and its story is indeed a "noble fiction" that teaches lessons to its readers. But the story of Atlantis has been so long remembered and is still so popular for another reason. The story of Atlantis has spoken subliminally

and powerfully to generations of human beings because it embodies mythic themes.

The Mythic Themes of Atlantis

Two great mythic themes in the Atlantis story are
those of paradise lost and of the flood. Both themes
appear in biblical stories—about Eden and Noah's
flood—and in myths and legends all over the world.
But in the Atlantis story they are combined and cen-
tered upon the fabulous lost land in the Atlantic
Ocean.

The Geography of Atlantis. All myths are
about the human condition, so the central figure in
every myth is humanity. The story of Atlantis seems
to be about a place, rather than about a person, but
the land can be seen as a symbolic embodiment of
humankind. There are indications within the story of
just such symbolism. For example, the layout of the
royal palace, as sketched above, involves a central
round island encircled by alternating rings of water
and land. The plan is that of a mandala at whose
center is a temple to the god who is the divine source
of the land. It is a diagram of the human soul, with
the divine spark in the middle encircled by its medi-
ating sheaths.

Plato's view of the geography of Earth is also
mythically symbolic of the human constitution. He
describes the world as a vast "true" continent in the
midst of which is an ocean that has two lesser island
continents in it. One island continent consists of
Europe, Africa, and Asia as its three parts, and the

other to the west is Atlantis. A land in the western ocean is found in many mythologies—for example, the Celtic—generally as the country of the dead.

The "true" continent that encloses everything is like the true Self, within which the illusion of separate selves is created, as the seemingly separate island continents are created by the waters of the ocean. One of those island continents is the ordinary world or everyday self that we identify with: the Europe-Africa-Asia we experience. The other is the subliminal self that survives death, but of which we know nothing because it has sunk beneath the surface of consciousness: the mysterious Atlantis.

Paradise Lost. If we think of Atlantis and its royal capital as representing the human constitution, then the story of Atlantis is the story of Eden. The land was populated by the god of the ocean. It was an ideal place, perfectly ruled and richly fruitful. But Atlantis fell from its happy state through greed and ambition, which led its inhabitants to ignore the divinely given laws, and so the land was consequently destroyed by earthquakes and floods sent by Zeus, the father of the gods.

This mythic story is strikingly similar in its essential point to that of Adam and Eve, who broke the divine commandment given to them and were led by greed and the ambition of being like God to eat the fruit of the Tree of Knowledge. As a result they were expelled from Paradise, whose gates were locked to them forever afterwards.

The theme of Paradise Lost has held great appeal because many of us have the feeling that we are strangers, lost in a strange land to which we have been exiled because our original home has been denied to us as a result of our greed for experience in the world. Life is then a quest to regain Paradise, to find the way back to Eden, to discover the path to the kingdom of Shambhala, to locate the lost Atlantis. Atlantis, like Eden and Shambhala, represents our first home, our source, our ground of being, which we have lost and which we long to recover.

The Flood. Stories of a great Flood are sometimes thought to be historical recollections of actual floods in primeval times. And physical floods undoubtedly enter into the mythic complex of the archetypal Flood. But human beings have not responded to the myth for so long all over the world simply because some of their ancestors were once caught in rising water on a river bank or the seashore. The theme of the Flood deals with psychological, not meteorological reality. Like any great mythic element, the Flood has many meanings; it speaks on many levels in many ways and cannot be reduced to only one of them.

One way of thinking about the Flood, however, is to say that each of us is an island of personal consciousness in the ocean of impersonal life. We are constantly threatened by the quakes of passion and the rising waters of the unconscious. There is a natural impulse within us to sustain our personal identities, it being our evolutionary goal to develop our separate selves in a manner harmonious with all other separate selves. So the spectacle of dry land being overwhelmed by water reminds us of the danger that our consciousness may be lost in the unconscious and our evolutionary purpose be frustrated or retarded.

The History of the Myth

Because of the power of the Atlantis story—only a few of whose mythic values have been touched on above—it has lived from the time Plato first told it until our own day. In the course of that long life, it has undergone many transformations. It was often referred to in the ancient classical world, though generally lost sight of during the Medieval period. After the revival of classical learning in the Renaissance, Atlantis came again into its own. The discovery of America especially resparked interest, for Plato had spoken of a continent lying beyond Atlantis, to the west of the Ocean. Since the nineteenth century, interest in Atlantis has again flourished. Here it is possible to mention only several of the main examples of that interest.

Donnelly's Antediluvian World. In the late nineteenth century, concern about Atlantis was particularly intensified, and its lore was turned to a new direction by Ignatius Donnelly. He was a lawyer and politician who had an interest in research and mysteries. After having served for a time as lieutenant governor of Minnesota, he went to Washington as a member of Congress. There he discovered the resources of the Library of Congress, and spent much time reading and storing away odd facts. Having served in the House of Representatives for eight years, Donnelly retired to his home and began to write books.

Donnelly's first book, published in 1882, was *Atlantis: The Antediluvian World*. It became immensely popular and molded the course of much of the later interest in the Atlantis story. Donnelly's thesis and his contribution to the Atlantis myth goes like this: There was once a physical connection between the eastern and western continents. This hypothesis best explains, or is the only way to explain, the similarities between the flora, fauna, and human cultures of the Americas and those of Europe, Africa, and Asia. Donnelly supposed the connection between east and west to be Plato's Atlantis—an island continent in the Atlantic Ocean, where human civilization began and from which it spread east and west as the Atlanteans extended themselves in a vast empire until the destruction of their homeland.

Donnelly's arguments excited a good deal of interest and respect when he made them. Today, however, they would be dismissed by almost all scientists and scholars as the result of overgeneralization, exaggeration, and unsupported imagination. Donnelly supposed that similarities have to be explained by a common historical origin, whereas various other explanations are possible. Furthermore, many of the similarities he found are superficial matters, and he ignored evidence that did not fit his theory. But Donnelly's contribution to the Atlantis myth was important, because by identifying Atlantis as a main source of human culture, he intensified its mythic value. In the Donnelly version, Atlantis was the place of origin of modern humanity, so its disappearance was all the more poignant, involving the loss of our homeland.

Blavatsky's Atlantis. H. P. Blavatsky, the great esotericist of the nineteenth century, referred casually to Plato's Atlantis several times in *Isis Unveiled* (1877), mainly to contrast the wisdom of the ancients with the skepticism of the moderns—a favorite theme of that book. In one reference (1:591), however, she speaks of Plato's account as containing "guarded hints . . . cleverly combining truth and fiction," thus clearly indicating that she did not regard the Platonic account as literal history, although she thought it contained deep and important truths.

By the time Blavatsky published *The Secret Doctrine* (1888), Donnelly's work was well known, and so she refers to his book as "that wonderful volume" (2: 266n) and cites him favorably a number of times. Blavatsky found Donnelly sympathetic because of his respect for the ancients and because he proposed an antiquity and distribution of civilization that went far beyond the limited Eurocentric views that most Europeans of her day assumed—and many of our day still do. Yet Blavatsky's Atlantis was quite different from Donnelly's.

In *The Secret Doctrine* Blavatsky developed a vast history of humanity, beginning not merely in prehistorical times, but even in prephysical states of being. Human history during our evolutionary cycle, according to Blavatsky, began in matter subtler than that we know and comprises seven great evolutionary stages, of which we are now in the fifth, which began about a million years ago. Each of the evolutionary stages (called "Root Races") is associated with a "continent" or configuration of land masses on the surface of the earth.

Blavatsky's "continents" can be compared with present-day theories of continental drift. Modern geologists believe the earth's land surfaces were once a single mass (called "Pangaea") that split into two. The southern half of Pangaea ("Gondwanaland") combined modern South America, Africa, Arabia, India, Australia, and Antarctica. The northern half ("Laurasia") later divided into North America and Eurasia, thus creating the Atlantic Ocean between them. The movement of land masses over the surface of the earth, according to modern theory, transforms the pattern of the continents through time, and thus produces shifting distributions of land not unlike Blavatsky's continents.

To the various "continents" and "Root Races" Blavatsky gave names which she borrowed from ancient traditions or modern speculations that she found congenial in spirit. *Lemuria* is the term she used for the "continent" of the third "Root Race." That name had been used in 1864 by the zoologist Philip L. Sclater for a hypothetical continent stretching from Africa to India and the Malay Peninsula. It is derived from *lemur,* signifying the monkey-like animal now found mainly in Madagascar but once more widely distributed in the Indian Ocean area. The continent was proposed to explain geological and zoological similarities in the area, which corresponds to part of Gondwanaland, a more recent scientific hypothesis.

To the "continent" of the fourth "Root Race"—the human evolutionary stage immediately preceding our own—Blavatsky gave the name *Atlantis*. In using the name, she clearly did not identify the fourth "continent" with Plato's island, nor with Donnelly's interpretation of it. What Blavatsky calls "Atlantis" is much older and larger than Plato's island. It is more nearly the configuration of land masses on the surface of our planet five to six million years ago, rather than a large island in the present Atlantic Ocean about 11,500 years ago. It is roughly comparable to, although not of the same geological age as, the modern concept of Laurasia.

Although Blavatsky may have thought that Plato's Atlantis preserved some distant hints of the land masses she called Atlantis, she certainly did not think they were the same thing. To suppose that Blavatsky was talking about the Platonic Atlantis because she used the name is a mistake, which can be avoided by reading what she said about the place she called by Plato's name.

Scott-Elliot's Atlantis.   W. Scott-Elliot wrote two books, *The Story of Atlantis* (1896) and *The Lost Lemuria* (1904) which are interesting efforts to combine and harmonize several traditions of the Atlantis myth. He views both continents within the Blavatsky tradition as the land masses on which earlier evolutionary stages of humanity lived. But he approaches their description very much in the Donnelly tradition by arguing that the historical distribution of certain features, natural and cultural, require the earlier existence of linking land masses. He cites scientific opinions of his day in support of that argument.

In addition, however, Scott-Elliot depended on the results of clairvoyant investigation into prehistory to supply details about the existence of those places and of human life in them. Such clairvoyance involves the use of faculties inherent in all human beings but under the active control of only a few. The person who controls and can use such faculties in a practical way perceives, through channels other than seeing or hearing, events at a distance in space and time. Both common experience and some scientific experimentation suggest that such faculties do indeed exist. Yet they are difficult to control and their results are hard to interpret.

If ordinary observation with eyes and ears is often mistaken or misleading, clairvoyant observation by subtler faculties is even less reliable. Clairvoyants must interpret what they perceive both for themselves and for others in terms that are familiar and recognizable. But the method of perception and often the things perceived are strikingly different from the ordinary. Clairvoyance, while real, is full of pitfalls, as Blavatsky pointed out, and should be interpreted with caution and a healthy dose of skepticism.

Although the clairvoyant source of Scott-Elliot's information about Atlantis and Lemuria is not identified in his book, it was almost certainly Charles Webster Leadbeater. Leadbeater was a Church of England clergyman who became an influential Theosophical writer. He was a remarkable clairvoyant whose hallmark was a highly detailed and physical-like interpretation of what he perceived. Leadbeater's accounts of primordial times, extraterrestrial places, cosmic patterns, infra-microscopic details, and worlds composed of rarefied matter made them seem as familiar and normal as one's own neighborhood or the bric-a-brac on a Victorian whatnot shelf. Leadbeater's descriptions were clear, easy to understand, specific, and concrete, even when he was dealing with the exotic and abstract. Consequently he became and remains today a widely read authority on the inner worlds. During 1894 he was engaged in clairvoyant research that led to the maps and some of the details of Scott-Elliot's book.

Scott-Elliot's descriptions of Lemuria and Atlantis combine Blavatsky's use of those terms for primordial land masses, a Donnelly-like argument from science which is now largely outdated, and Leadbeater's clairvoyant investigations of details of geography and culture. Thus Scott-Elliot brought together several traditions of Atlantology from the last century. His writing on the subject is a significant document in the history of Atlantis studies that began 2500 years ago.

In addition to its historical value as a phase in the development of the Atlantis myth, Scott-Elliot's compilation of Atlantis lore has its own intrinsic worth, as does his story of Lemuria. Myths are timeless. They satisfy human needs and appeal to our longing for explanations and guidance in a world we only imperfectly understand. Scott-Elliot treated these myths as myths need to be treated—not as a museum piece or a bit of curious antique lore, but as a living, literal reality.

To be effective, myths must be believed in. And paradoxically, believing in a myth makes it real. Atlantis is real because people have believed in it for two and a half millennia. The Atlantis myth and that of Lemuria are effective because they objectify deep-seated fears, hopes, longings, and expectations. We have all been denizens of the lost Atlantis. We are all Atlanteans who survived the flood. Scott-Elliot's book is a travel guide to our ancient homeland, now lost and sunk beneath the waves. Through this book we can visit in imagination the land of our mythic past and walk once again the streets of the City of the Golden Gates and see face to face the guardians of that land—the Masters of the Wisdom, who are both our past and our future.

Preface to the First Edition
A. P. SINNETT

For readers unacquainted with the progress that has been made in recent years by earnest students of occultism attached to the Theosophical Society, the significance of the statement embodied in the following pages would be misapprehended without some preliminary explanation. Historical research has depended for western civilization hitherto, on written records of one kind or another. When literary memoranda have fallen short, stone monuments have sometimes been available, and fossil remains have given us a few unequivocal, though inarticulate assurances concerning the antiquity of the human race; but modern culture has lost sight of or has overlooked possibilities connected with the investigation of past events, which are independent of fallible evidence transmitted to us by ancient writers. The world at large is thus at present so imperfectly alive to the resources of human faculty, that by most people as yet, the very existence, even as a potentiality, of psychic powers, which some of us all the while are consciously exercising every day, is scornfully denied and derided. The situation is sadly ludicrous

xxviii   *Preface*

from the point of view of those who appreciate the prospects of evolution, because mankind is thus wilfully holding at arm's length, the knowledge that is essential to its own ulterior progress. The maximum cultivation of which the human intellect is susceptible while it denies itself all the resources of its higher spiritual consciousness, can never be more than a preparatory process as compared with that which may set in when the faculties are sufficiently enlarged to enter into conscious relationship with the super-physical planes or aspects of Nature.

For anyone who will have the patience to study the published results of psychic investigation during the last fifty years, the reality of clairvoyance as an occasional phenomenon of human intelligence must establish itself on an immovable foundation. For those who, without being occultists—students that is to say of Nature's loftier aspects, in a position to obtain better teaching than that which any written books can give—for those who merely avail themselves of recorded evidence, a declaration on the part of others of a disbelief in the possibility of clairvoyance, is on a level with the proverbial African's disbelief in ice. But the experiences of clairvoyance that have accumulated on the hands of those who have studied it in connection with mesmerism, do no more than prove the existence in human nature of a capacity for cognizing physical phenomena distant either in space or time, in some way which has nothing to do with the physical senses. Those who have studied the mysteries of clairvoyance in connection with theosophic teaching have been enabled to realize that the ultimate resources of that faculty range as far beyond its humbler manifestations, dealt with by unassisted enquirers, as the resources of the higher mathematics exceed those of the abacus. Clairvoyance, indeed, is of many kinds, all of which fall easily into their places when we appreciate the manner in which human consciousness functions on different planes of Nature. The faculty of reading the pages of a closed book, or of discerning objects blindfold, or at a distance from the observer, is quite a different faculty from that employed on the cognition of past events. That last is the kind of which it is necessary to say something here, in order that the true character of the present treatise on Atlantis may be understood, but I allude to the others merely that the explanation I have to give may not be mistaken for a complete theory of clairvoyance in all its varieties.

We may best be helped to a comprehension of clairvoyance as related to past events, by considering in the first instance the phenomena of memory. The theory of memory which relates it to an imaginary rearrangement of physical molecules of brain matter, going on at every instant of our lives, is one that presents itself as plausible to no one who can ascend one degree above the thinking level of the uncompromising atheistical materialist. To every one who accepts, even as a reasonable hypothesis, the idea that a man is something more than a carcase in a state of animation, it must be a reasonable hypothesis that memory has to do with that principle in man which is super-physical. His memory in short, is a function of some other than the physical plane. The pictures of memory are imprinted, it is clear, on some non-physical medium, and are accessible to the embodied thinker in ordinary cases by virtue of some effort he makes in as much unconsciousness as to its precise character, as he is unconscious of the brain impulse which actuates the muscles of his heart. The events with which he has had to do in the past are photographed by Nature on some imperishable page of super-physical matter, and by making an appropriate interior effort, he is capable of bringing them again, when he requires them, within the area of some interior sense which reflects its perception on the physical brain. We are not all of us able to make this effort equally well, so that memory is sometimes dim, but even in the experience of mesmeric research, the occasional super-excitation of memory under mesmerism is a familiar fact. The circumstances plainly show that the record of Nature is accessible if we know how to recover it, or even if our own capacity to make an effort for its recovery is somehow improved without our having an improved knowledge of the method employed. And from this thought we may arrive by an easy transition at the idea, that in truth the records of Nature are not separate collections of individual property, but constitute the all-embracing memory of Nature herself, on which different people are in a position to make drafts according to their several capacities.

I do not say that the one thought necessarily ensues as a logical consequence of the other. Occultists know that what I have stated is the fact, but my present purpose is to show the reader who is not an Occultist, how the accomplished Occultist arrives at his results, without hoping to epitomize all the stages of his mental progress in this brief explanation. Theosophical literature at large must be consulted by those who would seek a fuller elucidation of the magnificent prospects and practical demonstrations of its teaching in many directions, which, in the course of the Theosophical development, have been laid before the world for the benefit of all who are competent to profit by them.

The memory of Nature is in reality a stupendous unity, just as in another way all mankind is found to constitute a spiritual unity if we ascend to a sufficiently elevated plane of Nature in search of the wonderful convergence where unity is reached without the loss of individuality. For ordinary humanity, however, at the early stage of its evolution represented at present by the majority, the interior spiritual capacities ranging beyond those which the brain is an instrument for expressing, are as yet too imperfectly developed to enable them to get into touch with any other records in the vast archives of Nature's memory, except those with which they have individually been in contact at their creation. The blindfold interior effort they are competent to make, will not as a rule, call up any others. But in a flickering fashion we have experience in ordinary life of efforts that are a little more effectual. ''Thought Transference'' is a humble example. In that case ''impressions on the mind'' of one person—Nature's memory pictures, with which he is in normal relationship, are caught up by someone else who is just able, however unconscious of the method he uses, to range Nature's memory under favourable conditions, a little beyond the area with which he himself is in normal relationship. Such a person has begun, however slightly, to exercise the faculty of astral clairvoyance. That term may be conveniently used to denote the kind of clairvoyance I am now endeavoring to elucidate, the kind which, in some of its more magnificent developments, has been employed to carry out the investigations on the basis of which the present account of Atlantis has been compiled.

There is no limit really to the resources of astral clairvoyance in investigations concerning the past history of the earth, whether we are concerned with the events that have befallen the human race in prehistoric epochs, or with the growth of the planet itself through geological periods which antedated the advent of man, or with more recent events, current narrations of which have been distorted by careless or perverse historians. The memory of Nature is infallibly accurate and inexhaustibly minute. A time will come as certainly as the precession of the equinoxes, when the literary method of historical research will be laid aside as out of date, in the case of all original work. People among us who are capable of exercising astral clairvoyance in full perfection— but have not yet been called away to higher functions in connection with the promotion of human progress, of which ordinary humanity at present knows even less than an Indian ryot knows of cabinet councils—are still very few. Those who know what the few can do, and through what processes of training and self-discipline they have passed in pursuit of interior ideals, of which when attained astral clairvoyance is but an individual circumstance, are many, but still a small minority as compared with the modern cultivated world. But as time goes on, and within a measurable future, some of us have reason to feel sure that the numbers of those who are competent to exercise astral clairvoyance will increase sufficiently to extend the circle of those who are aware of their capacities, till it comes to embrace all the intelligence and culture of civilized mankind only a few generations hence. Meanwhile the present volume is the first that has been put forward as the pioneer essay of the new method of historical research. It is amusing to all who are concerned with it, to think how inevitably it will be mistaken—for some little while as yet, by materialistic readers, unable to accept the frank explanation here given of the principle on which it has been prepared—for a work of imagination.

For the benefit of others who may be more intuitive it may be well to say a word or two that may guard them from supposing that because historical research by means of astral clairvoyance is not impeded by having to deal with periods removed from our own by hundreds of thousands of years, it is on that account a process which involves no trouble. Every fact stated in the present volume has been picked up bit by bit with watchful and attentive care, in the course of an investigation on which more than one qualified person has been engaged, in the intervals of other activity, for some years past. And to promote the success of their work they have been allowed access to some maps and other records physically preserved from the remote periods concerned —though in safer keeping than in that of the turbulent races occupied in Europe with the development of civilization in brief intervals of leisure from warfare, and hard pressed by the fanaticism that so long treated science as sacrilegious during the middle ages of Europe.

Laborious as the task has been however, it will be recognized as amply repaying the trouble taken, by everyone who is able to perceive how absolutely necessary to a proper comprehension of the world as we find it, is a proper comprehension of its preceding Atlantean phase. Without this knowledge all speculations concerning ethnology are futile and misleading. The course of race development is chaos and confusion without the key furnished by the character of Atlantean civilization and the configuration of the earth at Atlantean periods. Geologists know that land and ocean surfaces must have repeatedly changed places during the period at which they also know—from the situation of human remains in the various strata—that the lands were inhabited. And yet for want of accurate knowledge as to the dates at which the changes took place, they discard the whole theory from their practical thinking, and, except for certain hypotheses started by naturalists dealing with the southern hemisphere, have generally endeavoured to harmonize race migrations with the configuration of the earth in existence at the present time.

In this way nonsense is made of the whole retrospect; and the ethnological scheme remains so vague and shadowy that it fails to displace crude conceptions of mankind's beginning, which still dominate religious thinking and keep back the spiritual progress of the age. The decadence and ultimate disappearance of Atlantean civilization is in turn as instructive as its rise and glory; but I have now accomplished the main purpose with which I sought leave to introduce the work now before the world, with a brief prefatory explanation, and if its contents fail to convey a sense of its importance to any readers I am now addressing, that result could hardly be accomplished by further recommendations of mine.

1896

The Story of Atlantis
A Geographical, Historical and Ethnological Sketch

THE GENERAL scope of the subject before us will best be realized by considering the amount of information that is obtainable about the various nations who compose our great Fifth or Aryan Race.

From the time of the Greeks and the Romans onwards volumes have been written about every people who in their turn have filled the stage of history. The political institutions, the religious beliefs, the social and domestic manners and customs have all been analyzed and catalogued, and countless works in many tongues record for our benefit the march of progress.

Further, it must be remembered that of the history of this Fifth Race we possess but a fragment— the record merely of the last family races of the Celtic sub-race, and the first family races of our own Teutonic stock.

But the hundreds of thousands of years which elapsed from the time when the earliest Aryans left their home on the shores of the central Asian Sea to the time of the Greeks and Romans, bore witness to the rise and fall of innumerable civilizations. Of the 1st sub-race of our Aryan Race who inhabited India and colonized Egypt in prehistoric times we know practically nothing, and the same may be said of the Chaldean, Babylonian, and Assyrian nations who composed the 2nd sub-race—for the fragments of knowledge obtained from the recently deciphered hieroglyphs or cuneiform inscriptions on Egyptian tombs or Babylonian tablets can scarcely be said to constitute history. The Persians who belonged to the 3rd or Iranian sub-race have, it is true, left a few more traces, but of the earlier civilizations of the Celtic or 4th sub-race we have no records at all. It is only with the rise of the last family shoots of this Celtic stock, *viz.*, the Greek and Roman peoples, that we come upon historic times.

In addition also to the blank period in the past, there is the blank period in the future. For of the seven sub-races required to complete the history of a great Root Race, five only have so far come into existence. Our own Teutonic or 5th sub-race has already developed many nations, but has not yet run its course, while the 6th and 7th sub-races, who will be developed on the continents of North and South America, respectively, will have thousands of years of history to give to the world.

In attempting, therefore, to summarize in a few pages information about the world's progress during a period which must have occupied at least as great a stretch of years as that above referred to, it should be realized how slight a sketch this must inevitably be.

A record of the world's progress during the period of the Fourth or Atlantean Race must embrace the history of many nations, and register the rise and fall of many civilizations.

Catastrophes, too, on a scale such as has not yet been experienced during the life of our present Fifth Race, took place on more than one occasion during the progress of the Fourth. The destruction of Atlantis was accomplished by a series of catastrophes varying in character from great cataclysms in which whole territories and populations perished, to comparatively unimportant landslips such as occur on our own coasts to-day. When the destruction was once inaugurated by the first great catastrophe there was no intermission in the minor landslips which continued slowly but steadily to eat away the continent. Four of the great catastrophes stand out above the rest in magnitude. The first took place in the Miocene age, about 800,000 years ago. The second, which was of minor importance, occurred about 200,000 years ago. The third—about 80,000 years ago—was a very great one. It destroyed all that remained of the Atlantean continent, with the exception of the island to which Plato gave the name of Poseidonis, which in its turn was submerged in the fourth and final great catastrophe of 9564 B.C.

Now the testimony of the oldest writers and of modern scientific research alike bear witness to the existence of an ancient continent occupying the site of the lost Atlantis.

Before proceeding to the consideration of the subject itself, it is proposed cursorily to glance at the generally known sources which supply corroborative evidence. These may be grouped into the five following classes:

First, the testimony of the deep-sea surroundings.

Second, the distribution of fauna and flora.

Third, the similarity of language and of ethnological type.

Fourth, the similarity of religious belief, ritual, and architecture.

Fifth, the testimony of ancient writers, of early race traditions, and of archaic flood-legends.

Deep-Sea Soundings

In the first place, then, the testimony of the deep-sea soundings may be summarized in a few words. Thanks chiefly to the expeditions of the British and American gun boats, "Challenger" and "Dolphin" (though Germany also was associated in this scientific exploration) the bed of the whole Atlantic Ocean is now mapped out, with the result that an immense bank or ridge of great elevation is shown to exist in mid-Atlantic. This ridge stretches in a southwesterly direction from about fifty degrees north towards the coast of South America, then in a south-easterly direction towards the coast of Africa, changing its direction again about Ascension Island, and running due south to Tristan d'Acunha. The ridge rises almost sheer about 9,000 feet from the ocean depths around it, while the Azores, St. Paul, Ascension, and Tristan d'Acunha are the peaks of this land which still remain above water. A line of 3,500 fathoms, or say 21,000 feet, is required to sound the deepest parts of the Atlantic, but the higher parts of the ridge are only a hundred to a few hundred fathoms beneath the sea.

The soundings too showed that the ridge is covered with volcanic *débris* of which traces are to be found right across the ocean to the American coasts. Indeed the fact that the ocean bed, particularly about the Azores, has been the scene of volcanic disturbance on a gigantic scale, and that too within a quite measurable period of geologic time, is conclusively proved by the investigations made during the above-named expeditions.

Mr. Starkie Gardner is of opinion that in the Eocene times the British Islands formed part of a larger island or continent stretching into the Atlantic, and "that a great tract of land formerly existed where the sea now is, and that Cornwall, the Scilly and Channel Islands, Ireland and Brittany are the remains of its highest summits."*

Distribution of Fauna and Flora

The proved existence on continents separated by great oceans of similar or identical species of fauna and flora is the standing puzzle to biologists and botanists alike. But if a link between these continents once existed allowing for the natural migration of such animals and plants, the puzzle is solved. Now the fossil remains of the camel are found in India, Africa, South America and Kansas: but it is one of the generally accepted hypotheses of naturalists that every species of animal and plant originated in but one part of the globe, from which centre it gradually overran the other portions. How then can the facts of such fossil remains be accounted for without the existence of land communication in some remote age? Recent discoveries in the fossil beds of Nebraska seem also to prove that the horse

*Pop. Sc. Review, July, 1878.

originated in the Western Hemisphere, for that is the only part of the world where fossil remains have been discovered, showing the various intermediate forms which have been identified as the precursors of the true horse. It would therefore be difficult to account for the presence of the horse in Europe except on the hypothesis of continuous land communication between the two continents, seeing that it is certain that the horse existed in a wild state in Europe and Asia before his domestication by man, which may be traced back almost to the stone age. Cattle and sheep as we now know them have an equally remote ancestry. Darwin finds domesticated cattle in Europe in the earliest part of the stone age, having long before developed out of wild forms akin to the buffalo of America. Remains of the cave-lion of Europe are also found in North America.

Turning now from the animal to the vegetable kingdom it appears that the greater part of the flora of the Miocene age in Europe—found chiefly in the fossil beds of Switzerland—exist at the present day in America, some of them in Africa. But the noteworthy fact about America is that while the greater proportion are to be found in the Eastern States, very many are wanting on the Pacific coast. This seems to show that it was from the Atlantic side that they entered the continent. Professor Asa Gray says that out of 66 genera and 155 species found in the forest east of the Rocky Mountains, only 31 genera and 78 species are found west of these heights.

But the greatest problem of all is the plantain or banana. Professor Kuntze, an eminent German botanist, asks, ''In what way was this plant'' (a native of tropical Asia and Africa) "which cannot stand a voyage through the temperate zone, carried to America?" As he points out, the plant is seedless, it cannot be propagated by cuttings, neither has it a tuber which could be easily transported. Its root is tree-like. To transport it special care would be required, nor could it stand a long transit. The only way in which he can account for its appearance in America is to suppose that it must have been transported by civilized man at a time when the polar regions had a tropical climate! He adds, "a cultivated plant which does not possess seeds must have been under culture for a *very long period* . . . it is perhaps fair to infer that these plants were cultivated as early as the beginning of the Diluvial period." Why, it may be asked, should not this inference take us back to still earlier times, and where did the civilization necessary for the plant's cultivation exist, or the climate and circumstances requisite for its transportation, unless there were at some time a link between the old world and the new?

Professor Wallace in his delightful *Island Life,* as well as other writers in many important works, has put forward ingenious hypotheses to account for the identity of flora and fauna on widely separated lands, and for their transit across the ocean, but all are unconvincing, and all break down at different points.

It is well known that wheat as we know it has never existed in a truly wild state, nor is there any evidence tracing its descent from fossil species. Five varieties of wheat were *already cultivated* in Europe in the stone age—one variety found in the "Lake Dwellings" being known as Egyptian wheat, from which Darwin argues that the Lake dwellers "either still kept up commercial intercourse with some southern people, or had originally proceeded as colonists from the south." He concludes that wheat, barley, oats, etc., are descended from various *species now extinct,* or so widely different as to escape identification, in which case he says: "Man must have cultivated cereals from an enormously remote period." The regions where these extinct species flourished, and the civilization under which they were cultivated by intelligent selection, are both supplied by the lost continent whose colonists carried them east and west.

From the fauna and flora we now turn to man.

Similarity of Language

The Basque language stands alone amongst European tongues, having affinity with none of them. According to Farrar, "there never has been any doubt that this isolated language, preserving its identity in a western corner of Europe, between two mighty kingdoms, resembles in its structure the aboriginal languages of the vast opposite continent (America) and those alone."*

The Phoenicians apparently were the first nation in the Eastern Hemisphere to use a phonetic alphabet, the characters being regarded as mere signs for sounds. It is a curious fact that at an equally early date we find a phonetic alphabet in Central America

*Families of Speech, p. 132.

amongst the Mayans of Yucatan, whose traditions ascribe the origin of their civilization to a land across the sea to the east. Le Plongeon, the great authority on this subject, writes: "One-third of this tongue (the Maya) is pure Greek. Who brought the dialect of Homer to America? or who took to Greece that of the Mayas? Greek is the offspring of the Sanscrit. Is Maya? or are they coeval?" Still more surprising is it to find thirteen letters out of the Maya alphabet bearing most distinct relation to the Egyptian hieroglyphic signs for the same letters. It is probable that the earliest form of alphabet was hieroglyphic, "the writing of the Gods," as the Egyptians called it, and that it developed later in Atlantis into the phonetic. It would be natural to assume that the Egyptians were an early colony from Atlantis (as they actually were) and that they carried away with them the primitive type of writing which has thus left its traces on both hemispheres, while the Phœnicians, who were a sea-going people, obtained and assimilated the later form of alphabet during their trading voyages with the people of the west.

One more point may be noticed, *viz.*, the extraordinary resemblance between many words in the Hebrew language and words bearing precisely the same meaning in the tongue of the Chiapenecs—a branch of the Maya race, and amongst the most ancient in Central America.*

The similarity of language among the various savage races of the Pacific islands has been used as an

*A list of these words is given in *North Americans of Antiquity*, p. 475.

argument by writers on this subject. The existences of similar languages among races separated by leagues of ocean, across which in historic time they are known to have had no means of transport, is certainly an argument in favour of their descent from a single race occupying a single continent, but the argument cannot be used here, for the continent in question was not Atlantis, but the still earlier Lemuria.

Similarity of Ethnological Types

Atlantis as we shall see is said to have been inhabited by red, yellow, white and black races. It is now proved by the researches of Le Plongeon, De Quatrefages, Bancroft and others that black populations of negroid type existed even up to recent times in America. Many of the monuments of Central America are decorated with negro faces, and some of the idols found there are clearly intended to represent negroes, with small skulls, short woolly hair and thick lips. The Popul Vuh, speaking of the first home of the Guatemalan race, says that "black and white men together" lived in this happy land "in great peace," speaking "one language."* The Popul Vuh goes on to relate how the people migrated from their ancestral home, how their language *became altered,* and how some went to the east, while others travelled west (to Central America).

*See Bancroft's *Native Races,* p. 547.

Professor Retzius, in his *Smithsonian Report,* considers that the primitive dolichocephalae of America are nearly related to the Guanches of the Canary Islands, and to the population on the Atlantic seaboard of Africa, which Latham comprises under the name of Egyptian Atlantidae. The same form of skull is found in the Canary Islands off the African coast and the Carib Islands off the American coast, while the colour of the skin in both is that of a reddish-brown.

The ancient Egyptians depicted themselves as red men of much the same complexion as exists to-day among some tribes of American Indians.

"The ancient Peruvians," says Short, "appear from numerous examples of hair found in their tombs to have been an auburn-haired race."

A remarkable fact about the American Indians, and one which is a standing puzzle to ethnologists, is the wide range of colour and complexion to be found among them. From the white tint of the Menominee, Dakota, Mandan, and Zuni tribes, many of whom have auburn hair and blue eyes, to the almost negro blackness of the Karos of Kansas and the now extinct tribes of California, the Indian races run through every shade of red-brown, copper, olive, cinnamon, and bronze.*

We shall see by and by how the diversity of com-

---

*See Short's *North Americans of Antiquity,* Winchell's *Pre-Adamites,* and Catlin's *Indians of North America;* see also *Atlantis,* by Ignatius Donnelly, who has collected a great mass of evidence under this and other heads.

plexion on the American Continent is accounted for by the original race-tints on the parent continent of Atlantis.

Similarity of Religious Belief, Ritual and Architecture

Nothing seems to have surprised the first Spanish adventurers in Mexico and Peru more than the extraordinary similarity to those of the old world, of the religious beliefs, rites, and emblems which they found established in the new. The Spanish priests regarded this similarity as the work of the devil. The worship of the cross by the natives, and its constant presence in all religious buildings and ceremonies, was the principal subject of their amazement; and indeed nowhere—not even in India and Egypt—was this symbol held in more profound veneration than amongst the primitive tribes of the American continents, while the meaning underlying its worship was identical. In the west, as in the east, the cross was the symbol of life—sometimes of life physical, more often of life eternal.

In like manner in both hemispheres the worship of the sun-disk or circle, and of the serpent, was universal, and more surprising still is the similarity of the word signifying "God" in the principal languages of east and west. Compare the Sanscrit "Dyaus" or "Dyaus-pitar," the Greek, "Theos" and Zeus, the Latin "Deus" and "Jupiter," the Keltic "Dia" and "Ta," pronounced "Thyah" (seeming to bear affinity to the Egyptian Tau), the Jewish "Jah" or "Yah" and lastly the Mexican "Teo" or "Zeo."

Baptismal rites were practised by all nations. In Babylon and Egypt the candidates for initiation in the Mysteries were first baptized. Tertullian in his *De Baptismo* says that they were promised in consequence "regeneration and the pardon of all their perjuries." The Scandinavian nations practised baptism of new-born children; and when we turn to Mexico and Peru we find infant baptism there as a solemn ceremonial, consisting of water sprinkling, the sign of the cross, and prayers for the washing away of sin.*†

In addition to baptism, the tribes of Mexico, Central America and Peru resembled the nations of the old world in their rites of confession, absolution, fasting, and marriage before priests by joining hands. They had even a ceremony resembling the Eucharist, in which cakes marked with the Tau (an Egyptian form of cross) were eaten, the people calling them the flesh of their God. These exactly resemble the sacred cakes of Egypt and other eastern nations. Like these nations, too, the people of the new world had monastic orders, male and female, in which broken vows were punished with death. Like the Egyptians they embalmed their dead, they worshipped sun, moon and planets, but over and above

*See Humboldt's *Mexican Researches* and Prescott's *Mexico.*
†For a fuller description of Baptismal Rites see W. Williamson's *"The Great Law,"* chap. "Sacraments and Blood Covenants."

these adored a Deity "omnipresent, who knoweth all things . . . invisible, incorporeal, one God of perfect perfection."*

They too had their virgin-mother goddess, "Our Lady" whose son, the "Lord of Light," was called the "Saviour," bearing an accurate correspondence to Isis, Beltis and the many other virgin-goddesses of the east with their divine sons.

Their rites of sun and fire worship closely resembled those of the early Celts of Britain and Ireland, and like the latter they claimed to be the "children of the sun." An ark or argha was one of the universal sacred symbols which we find alike in India, Chaldea, Assyria, Egypt, Greece and amongst the Celtic peoples. Lord Kingsborough in his *Mexican Antiquities*† says: "As among the Jews the ark was a sort of portable temple in which the deity was supposed to be continually present, so among the Mexicans, the Cherokees and the Indians of Michoacan and Honduras, an ark was held in the highest veneration and was considered an object too sacred to be touched by any but the priests."

As to religious architecture, we find on both sides of the Atlantic that one of the earliest sacred buildings is the pyramid. Doubtful as are the uses for which these structures were originally intended, one thing is clear, that they were closely connected with some religious idea or group of ideas. The identity of design in the pyramids of Egypt and those of Mexico

*See Sahagun's *Historia de Nueva España,* lib. vi.
†Vol. viii, p. 250.

and Central America is too striking to be a mere co-incidence. True some—the greater number—of the American pyramids are of the truncated or flattened form, yet according to Bancroft and others, many of those found in Yucatan, and notably those near Palenque, are pointed at the top in true Egyptian fashion, while on the other hand we have some of the Egyptian pyramids of the stepped and flattened type. Cholula has been compared to the groups of Dachour, Sakkara and the step pyramid of Médourn. Alike in orientation, in structure, and even in their internal galleries and chambers, these mysterious monuments of the east and of the west stand as witnesses to some common source whence their builders drew their plan.

The vast remains of cities and temples in Mexico and Yucatan also strangely resemble those of Egypt, the ruins of Teotihuacan having frequently been compared to those of Karnak. The "false arch"—horizontal courses of stone, each slightly overlapping the other—is found to be identical in Central America, in the oldest buildings of Greece, and in Etruscan remains. The mound builders of both eastern and western continents formed similar tumuli over their dead, and laid the bodies in similar stone coffins. Both continents have their great serpent-mounds; compare that of Adams Co., Ohio, with the fine serpent-mound discovered in Argyleshire, or the less perfect specimen at Avebury in Wilts. The very carving and decoration of the temples of America, Egypt and India have much in common, while some of the mural decorations are absolutely identical.

Testimony of Ancient Writers

It only remains now to summarize some of the evidence obtainable from ancient writers, from early race traditions, and from archaic flood-legends.

Aelian in his *Varia Historia,** states that Theopompus (400 B.C.) recorded an interview between the King of Phrygia and Silenus, in which the latter referred to the existence of a great continent beyond the Atlantic, larger than Asia, Europe and Libya together.

Proclus quotes an extract from an ancient writer who refers to the islands in the sea beyond the Pillars of Hercules (Straits of Gibraltar), and says that the inhabitants of one of these islands had a tradition from their ancestors of an extremely large island called Atlantis, which for a long time ruled over all the islands of the Atlantic Ocean.

Marcellus speaks of seven islands in the Atlantic, and states that their inhabitants preserve the memory of a much greater island, Atlantis, "which had for a long time exercised dominion over the smaller ones."

Diodorus Siculus relates that the Phœnicians discovered "a large island in the Atlantic Ocean beyond the Pillars of Hercules several days' sail from the coast of Africa."

But the greatest authority on this subject is Plato. In the *Timaeus* he refers to the island continent, while the *Critias* or *Atlanticus* is nothing less than a detailed account of the history, arts, manners and customs of

*Lib. iii., ch. xviii.

the people. In the *Timaeus* he refers to "a mighty warlike power, rushing from the Atlantic sea and spreading itself with hostile fury over all Europe and Asia. For at that time the Atlantic sea was navigable and had an island before that mouth which is called by you the Pillars of Hercules. But this island was greater than both Libya and all Asia together, and afforded an easy passage to other neighbouring islands, as it was likewise easy to pass from those islands to all the continents which border on this Atlantic sea."

There is so much of value in the *Critias* that it is not easy to choose, but the following extract is given, as it bears on the material resources of the country: "They had likewise everything provided for them which both in a city and every other place is sought after as useful for the purposes of life. And they were supplied indeed with many things from foreign countries, on account of their extensive empire; but the island afforded them the greater part of everything of which they stood in need. In the first place the island supplied them with such things as are dug out of mines in a solid state, and with such as are melted: and orichalcum, which is now but seldom mentioned, but then was much celebrated, was dug out of the earth in many parts of the island, and was considered as the most honourable of all metals except gold. Whatever, too, the woods afforded for builders the island produced in abundance. There were likewise sufficient pastures there for tame and savage animals; together with a prodigious number of elephants. For there were pastures for all such animals as are fed in lakes and rivers; on mountains and in plains. And in like manner there was sufficient aliment for the largest and most voracious kind of animals. Besides this, whatever of odoriferous the earth nourishes at present, whether roots, or grass, or wood, or juices, or gums, flowers or fruits—these the island produced and produced them well.''

The Gauls possessed traditions of Atlantis which were collected by the Roman historian, Timagenes, who lived in the first century, B.C. Three distinct peoples apparently dwelt in Gaul. First, the indigenous population (probably the remains of a Lemurian race), second, the invaders from the distant island of Atlantis, and third, the Aryan Gauls.*

The Toltecs of Mexico traced themselves back to a starting-point called Atlan or Aztlan; the Aztecs also claimed to come from Aztlan.†

The Popul Vuh‡ speaks of a visit paid by three sons of the King of the Quiches to a land ''in the east on the shores of the sea whence their fathers had come,'' from which they brought back amongst other things ''a system of writing.''§

Amongst the Indians of North America there is a very general legend that their forefathers came from a land ''toward the sun-rising.'' The Iowa and Dakota Indians, according to Major J. Lind, believed that ''all the tribes of Indians were formerly one and dwelt together *on an island* . . . towards the sunrise.'' They crossed the sea from thence ''in huge

---

*See *Pre-Adamites,* p. 380.
†See Bancroft's *Native Races,* vol. v. pp. 221 and 321.
‡Page 294.
§See also Bancroft, Vol. V., p. 553.

skiffs in which the Dakotas of old floated for weeks, finally gaining dry land.''

The Central American books state that a part of the American continent extended far into the Atlantic Ocean, and that this region was destroyed by a series of frightful cataclysms at long intervals apart. *Three* of these are frequently referred to.* It is a curious confirmation that the Celts of Britain had a legend that part of *their* country once extended far into the Atlantic and was destroyed. Three catastrophes are mentioned in the Welsh traditions.

Quetzalcoatl, the Mexican Deity, is said to have come from ''the distant east.'' He is described as a white man with a flowing beard. (N.B.—The Indians of North and South America are beardless.) He originated letters and regulated the Mexican calendar. After having taught them many peaceful arts and lessons he sailed away *to the east* in a canoe made of serpent skins.† The same story is told of Zamna, the author of civilization in Yucatan.

The marvellous uniformity of the flood legends on all parts of the globe, alone remains to be dealt with. Whether these are some archaic versions of the story of the lost Atlantis and its submergence, or whether they are echoes of a great cosmic parable once taught and held in reverence in some common centre whence they have reverberated throughout the world, does not immediately concern us. Sufficient for our purpose is it to show the universal acceptance of these legends. It would be needless waste of time and space

*See Baldwin's *Ancient America,* p. 176.
†See Short's *North Americans of Antiquity,* pp. 268-271.

to go over these flood stories one by one. Suffice it to say, that in India, Chaldea, Babylon, Media, Greece, Scandinavia, China, amongst the Jews and amongst the Celtic tribes of Britain, the legend is absolutely identical in all essentials. Now turn to the west and what do we find? The same story in its every detail preserved amongst the Mexicans (each tribe having its own version), the people of Guatemala, Honduras, Peru, and almost every tribe of North American Indians. It is puerile to suggest that mere coincidence can account for this fundamental identity.

The following quotation from Le Plongeon's translation of the famous Troano MS., which may be seen in the British Museum, will appropriately bring this part of the subject to a close. The Troano MS. appears to have been written about 3,500 years ago, among the Mayas of Yucatan, and the following is its description of the catastrophe that submerged the island of Poseidonis:—"In the year 6 Kan, on the 11th Muluc in the month Zac, there occurred terrible earthquakes, which continued without interruption until the 13th Chuen. The country of the hills of mud, the land of Mu was sacrificed: being twice upheaved it suddenly disappeared during the night, the basin being continually shaken by volcanic forces. Being confined, these caused the land to sink and to rise several times and in various places. At last the surface gave way and ten countries were torn asunder and scattered. Unable to stand the force of the convulsions, they sank with their 64,000,000 of inhabitants 8060 years before the writing of this book."

The Occult Records

But enough space has now been devoted to the fragments of evidence—all more or less convincing —which the world so far has been in possession of. Those interested in pursuing any special line of investigation are referred to the various works above named or quoted.

The subject in hand must now be dealt with. Drawn as they have been from contemporary records which were compiled in and handed down through the ages we have to deal with, the facts here collected are based upon no assumption or conjecture. The writer may have failed fully to comprehend the facts, and so may have partially misstated them. But the original records are open for investigation to the duly qualified, and those who are disposed to undertake the necessary training may obtain the powers to check and verify.

But even were *all* the occult records open to our inspection, it should be realized how fragmentary must be the sketch that attempts to summarize in a few pages the history of races and of nations extending over at least many hundreds of thousands of years. However, any details on such a subject—disconnected though they are—must be new, and should therefore be interesting to the world at large.

Among the records above referred to there are maps of the world at various periods of its history and it has been the great privilege of the writer to be allowed to obtain copies—more or less complete—of four of these. All four represent Atlantis and the surrounding lands at different epochs of their history.

These epochs correspond approximately with the periods that lay between the catastrophes referred to above, and into the periods thus represented by the four maps the records of the Atlantean Race will naturally group themselves.

First Map Period

Before beginning the history of the race, however, a few remarks may be made about the geography of the four different epochs.

The first map represents the land surface of the earth as it existed about a million years ago, when the Atlantean Race was at its height, and before the first great submergence took place about 800,000 years ago. The continent of Atlantis itself, it will be observed, extended from a point a few degrees east of Iceland to about the site now occupied by Rio de Janeiro, in South America. Embracing Texas and the Gulf of Mexico, the Southern and Eastern States of America, up to and including Labrador, it stretched across the ocean to our own islands—Scotland and Ireland, and a small portion of the north of England forming one of its promontories—while its equatorial lands embraced Brazil and the whole stretch of ocean to the African Gold Coast. Scattered fragments of what eventually became the continents of Europe, Africa and America, as well as remains of the still older, and once widespread continent of Lemuria, are also shown on this map. The remains of the still older Hyperborean continent which was inhabited by the Second Root Race, are also given, and like Lemuria, coloured blue.

Second Map Period

As will be seen from the second map the catastrophe of 800,000 years ago caused very great changes in the land distribution of the globe. The great continent is now shorn of its northern regions, and its remaining portion has been still further rent. The now growing American continent is separated by a chasm from its parent continent of Atlantis, and this no longer comprises any of the lands now existing, but occupies the bulk of the Atlantic basin from about 50° north to a few degrees south of the equator. The subsidences and upheavals in other parts of the world have also been considerable—the British Islands for example, now being part of a huge island which also embraces the Scandinavian peninsula, the North of France, and all the intervening and some of the surrounding seas. The dimensions of the remains of Lemuria it will be observed, have been further curtailed, while Europe, Africa and America have received accretions of territory.

Third Map Period

The third map shows the results of the catastrophe which took place about 200,000 years ago. With the exception of the rents in the continents both of Atlantis and America, and the submergence of Egypt, it will be seen how relatively unimportant were the subsidences and upheavals at this epoch, indeed the fact that this catastrophe has not always been considered as one of the great ones, is apparent from the quotation already given from the sacred book of the Guatemalans—three great ones only being there mentioned. The Scandinavian island however, appears now as joined to the mainland. The two islands into which Atlantis was now split were known by the names of Ruta and Daitya.

Fourth Map Period

The stupendous character of the natural convulsion that took place about 80,000 years ago, will be apparent from the fourth map. Daitya, the smaller and more southerly of the islands, has almost entirely disappeared, while of Ruta there only remains the relatively small island of Poseidonis. This map was compiled about 75,000 years ago, and it no doubt fairly represents the land surface of the earth from that period onwards till the final submergence of Poseidonis in 9564 B.C., though during that period minor changes must have taken place. It will be noted that the land outlines had then begun to assume roughly the same appearance they do to-day, though the British Islands were still joined to the European continent, while the Baltic Sea was non-existent, and the Sahara desert then formed part of the ocean floor.

The Manus

Some reference to the very mystical subject of the Manus is a necessary preliminary to the consideration of the origin of a Root Race. In Transaction No. 26, of the London Lodge, reference was made to the work done by these very exalted Beings, which embraces not only the planning of the types of the whole Manvantara, but the superintending the formation and education of each Root Race in turn. The following quotation refers to these arrangements: ''There are also Manus whose duty it is to act in a similar way for each Root Race on each Planet of the Round, the Seed Manu planning the improvement in type which each successive Root Race inaugurates, and the Root Manu actually incarnating amongst the new Race as a leader and teacher to direct the development and ensure the improvement.''

The way in which the necessary segregation of the picked specimens is effected by the Manu in charge, and his subsequent care of the growing community, may be dealt with in a future Transaction. The merest reference to the mode of procedure is all that is necessary here.

It was of course from one of the sub-races of the Third Root Race on the continent which is spoken of as Lemuria, that the segregation was effected which was destined to produce the Fourth Root Race.

Following where necessary the history of the Race through the four periods represented by the four maps, it is proposed to divide the subject under the following headings:

1. Origin and territorial location of the different sub-races.

2. The political institutions they respectively evolved.

3. Their emigrations to other parts of the world.

4. The arts and sciences they developed.

5. The manners and customs they adopted.

6. The rise and decline amongst them of religious ideas.

The Sub-Races

The names of the different sub-races must first be given—

1. Rmoahal.   4. First Turanian.
2. Tlavatli.   5. Original Semite.
3. Toltec.   6. Akkadian.
            7. Mongolian.

Some explanation is necessary as to the principle on which these names are chosen. Wherever modern ethnologists have discovered traces of one of these sub-races, or even identified a small part of one, the name they have given to it is used for the sake of simplicity, but in the case of the first two sub-races there are hardly any traces left for science to seize upon, so the names by which they called themselves have been adopted.

The Rmoahal Race

Now the period represented by Map No. 1 shows the land surface of the earth as it existed about one mil-

lion years ago, but the Rmoahal race came into existence between four and five million years ago, at
which period large portions of the great southern
continent of Lemuria still existed, while the continent of Atlantis had not assumed the proportions it
ultimately attained. It was upon a spur of this
Lemurian land that the Rmoahal race was born.
Roughly it may be located at latitude 7° north and
longitude 5° west, which a reference to any modern
atlas will show to lie on the Ashanti coast of to-day. It
was a hot, moist country, where huge antediluvian
animals lived in reedy swamps and dank forests. The
Rmoahals were a dark race—their complexion being
a sort of mahogany black. Their height in these early
days was about ten or twelve feet—truly a race of
giants—but through the centuries their stature gradually dwindled, as did that of all the races in turn,
and later on we shall find they had shrunk to the stature of the "Furfooz man." They ultimately migrated to the southern shores of Atlantis, were they
were engaged in constant warfare with the sixth and
seventh sub-races of the Lemurians then inhabiting
that country. A large part of the tribe eventually
moved north, while the remainder settled down and
intermarried with these black Lemurian aborigines.
The result was that at the period we are dealing
with—the first map period—there was no pure blood
left in the south, and as we shall see it was from these
dark races who inhabited the equatorial provinces,
and the extreme south of the continent, that the
Toltec conquerors subsequently drew their supplies
of slaves. The remainder of the race, however,
reached the extreme north-eastern promontories
contiguous with Iceland, and dwelling there for un-

told generations, they gradually became lighter in colour, until at the date of the first map period we find them a tolerably fair people. Their descendants eventually became subject, at least nominally, to the Semite kings.

That they dwelt there for untold generations is not meant to imply that their occupation was unbroken, for stress of circumstances at intervals of time drove them south. The cold of the glacial epochs of course operated alike with the other races, but the few words to be said on this subject may as well come in here.

Without going into the question of the different rotations which this earth performs, or the varying degrees of eccentricity of its orbit, a combination of which is sometimes held to be the cause of the glacial epochs, it is a fact—and one already recognized by some astronomers—that a minor glacial epoch occurs about every 30,000 years. But in addition to these, there were two occasions in the history of Atlantis when the ice-belt desolated not merely the northern regions, but, invading the bulk of the continent, forced all life to migrate to equatorial lands. The first of these was in process during the Rmoahal days, about 3,000,000 years ago, while the second took place in the Toltec ascendency about 850,000 years ago.

With reference to all glacial epochs it should be stated that though the inhabitants of northern lands were forced to settle during the winter far south of the ice-belt, there yet were great districts to which in summer they could return, and where for the sake of the hunting they encamped until driven south again by the winter cold.

The Tlavatli Race

The place of origin of the Tlavatli or 2nd sub-race was an island off the west coast of Atlantis. The spot is marked on the 1st map with the figure 2. Thence they spread into Atlantis proper, chiefly across the middle of the continent, gradually however tending northwards towards the stretch of coast facing the promontory of Greenland. Physically they were a powerful and hardy race of a red-brown colour, but they were not quite so tall as the Rmoahals whom they drove still further north. They were always a mountain-loving people, and their chief settlements were in the mountainous districts of the interior, which a comparison of Maps 1 and 4 will show to be approximately coterminous with what ultimately became the island of Poseidonis. At this first map period they also—as just stated—peopled the northern coasts, whilst a mixture of Tlavatli and Toltec race inhabited the western islands, which subsequently formed part of the American continent.

The Toltec Race

We now come to the Toltec or 3rd sub-race. This was a magnificent development. It ruled the whole continent of Atlantis for thousands of years in great material power and glory. Indeed so dominant and so endowed with vitality was this race that intermarriages with the following sub-races failed to modify the type, which still remained essentially Toltec; and hundreds of thousands of years later we find one of their remote family races ruling magnificently in

Mexico and Peru, long ages before their degenerate
descendants were conquered by the fiercer Aztec
tribes from the north. The complexion of this race
was also a red-brown, but they were redder or more
copper-coloured than the Tlavatli. They also were a
tall race, averaging about eight feet during the
period of their ascendency, but of course dwindling,
as all races did, to the dimensions that are common
to-day. The type was an improvement on the two
previous sub-races, the features being straight and
well marked, not unlike the ancient Greek. The approximate birthplace of this race may be seen,
marked with the figure 3, on the first map. It lay
near the west coast of Atlantis about latitude 30°
North, and the whole of the surrounding country,
embracing the bulk of the west coast of the continent,
was peopled with a pure Toltec race. But as we shall
see when dealing with the political organization,
their territory eventually extended right across the
continent, and it was from their great capital on the
eastern coast that the Toltec emperors held their
almost world-wide sway.

The First Turanian Race

The Turanian or 4th sub-race had their origin on the
eastern side of the continent, south of the mountainous district inhabited by the Tlavatli people. This
spot is marked 4 on Map No. 1. The Turanians were
colonists from the earliest days, and great numbers
migrated to the lands lying to the east of Atlantis.

They were never a thoroughly dominant race on the mother-continent, though some of their tribes and family races became fairly powerful. The great central regions of the continent lying west and south of the Tlavatli mountainous district was their special though not their exclusive home, for they shared these lands with the Toltecs. The curious political and social experiments made by this sub-race will be dealt with later on.

The Original Semite Race

As regards the original Semite or 5th sub-race ethnologists have been somewhat confused, as indeed it is extremely natural they should be considering the very insufficient data they have to go upon. This sub-race had its origin in the mountainous country which formed the more southerly of the two north-eastern peninsulas which, as we have seen, is now represented by Scotland, Ireland, and some of the surrounding seas. The site is marked 5 in Map No. 1. In this least desirable portion of the great continent the race grew and flourished, for centuries maintaining its independence against aggressive southern kings, till the time came for it in turn to spread abroad and colonize. It must be remembered that by the time the Semites rose to power hundreds of thousands of years had passed and the 2nd map period had been reached. They were a turbulent, discontented race, always at war with their neighbours, especially with the then growing power of the Akkadians.

The Akkadian Race

The birthplace of the Akkadian or 6th sub-race will be found on Map No. 2 (marked there with the figure 6), for it was after the great catastrophe of 800,000 years ago that this race first came into existence. It took its rise in the land east of Atlantis, about the middle of the great peninsula whose southeastern extremity stretched out towards the old continent. The spot may be located approximately at latitude 42° North and longitude 10° East. They did not for long, however, confine themselves to the land of their birth, but overran the now diminished continent of Atlantis. They fought with the Semites in many battles both on land and sea, and very considerable fleets were used on both sides. Finally about 100,000 years ago they completely vanquished the Semites, and from that time onwards an Akkadian dynasty was set up in the old Semite capital, and ruled the country wisely for several hundred years. They were a great trading, sea-going and colonizing people, and they established many centres of communication with distant lands.

The Mongolian Race

The Mongolian or 7th sub-race seems to be the only one that had absolutely no touch with the mother-continent. Having its origin on the plains of Tartary (marked No. 7 on the second map) at about latitude 63° North and longitude 140° East, it was directly developed from descendants of the Turanian race, which it gradually supplanted over the greater part of Asia. This sub-race multiplied exceedingly, and even at the present day a majority of the earth's inhabitants technically belong to it, though many of its divisions are so deeply coloured with the blood of earlier races as to be scarcely distinguishable from them.

Political Institutions

In such a summary as this it would be impossible to describe how each sub-race was further sub-divided into nations, each having its distinct type and characteristics. All that can be here attempted is to sketch in broad outline the varying political institutions throughout the great epochs of the race.

While recognizing that each sub-race as well as each Root Race is destined to stand in some respects at a higher level than the one before it, the cyclic nature of the development must be recognized as leading the race like the man through the various phases of infancy, youth, and manhood back to the infancy of old age again. Evolution necessarily means ultimate progress, even though the turning back of its ascending spiral may seem to make the history of politics or of religion a record not merely of development and progress but also of degradation and decay.

In making the statement therefore that the 1st sub-race started under the most perfect government conceivable, it must be understood that this was owing to the necessities of their childhood, not to the merits of their matured manhood. For the Rmoahals were incapable of developing any plan of settled government, nor did they ever reach even as high a point of civilization as the 6th and 7th Lemurian sub-races. But the Manu who effected the segregation actually incarnated in the race and ruled it as king. Even when he no longer took visible part in the government of the race, Adept or Divine rulers were, when the times required it, still provided for the infant community. As students of *The Secret Doctrine* know, our humanity had not then reached the stage of development necessary to produce fully initiated Adepts. The rulers above referred to, including the Manu himself, were therefore necessarily the product of evolution on other systems of worlds.

The Tlavatli people showed some signs of advance in the art of government. Their various tribes or nations were ruled by chiefs or kings who generally received their authority by acclamation of the people. Naturally the most powerful individuals and greatest warriors were so chosen. A considerable empire was eventually established among them, in which one king became the nominal head, but his suzerainty consisted rather in titular honour than in actual authority.

It was the Toltec race who developed the highest civilization and organised the most powerful empire of any of the Atlantean peoples, and it was then that the principle of heredity succession was for the first time established. The race was at first divided into a number of petty independent kingdoms, constantly at war with each other, and all at war with the Lemurio-Rmoahals of the south. These were gradually conquered and made subject peoples—many of their tribes being reduced to slavery. About one million years ago, however, these separate kingdoms united in a great federation with a recognized emperor at its head. This was of course inaugurated by great wars, but the outcome was peace and prosperity for the race.

It must be remembered that humanity was still for the most part possessed of psychic attributes, and by this time the most advanced had undergone the necessary training in the occult schools, and had attained various stages of initiation—some even reaching to Adeptship. Now the second of these emperors was an Adept, and for thousands of years the Divine dynasty ruled not only all the kingdoms into which Atlantis was divided but the islands on the West and the southern portion of the adjacent land lying to the east. When necessary, this dynasty was recruited from the Lodge of Initiates, but as a rule the power was handed down from father to son, all being more or less qualified, and the son in some cases receiving a further degree at the hands of his father. During all this period these Initiate rulers retained connection with the Occult Hierarchy which governs the world, submitting to its laws, and acting in harmony with its plans. This was the golden age of the Toltec race. The government was just and beneficent; the arts and sciences were cultivated—indeed the workers in these fields, guided as they were by occult knowledge, achieved tremendous results; religious belief and ritual were still comparatively pure

—in fact the civilization of Atlantis had by this time reached its height.

Sorcery versus *the Good Law*

After about 100,000 years of this golden age the degeneracy and decay of the race set in. Many of the tributary kings, and large numbers of the priests and people ceased to use their faculties and powers in accordance with the laws made by their Divine rulers, whose precepts and advice were now disregarded. Their connection with the Occult Hierarchy was broken. Personal aggrandisement, the attainment of wealth and authority, the humiliation and ruin of their enemies became more and more the objects towards which their occult powers were directed: and thus turned from their lawful use, and practised for all sorts of selfish and malevolent purposes, they inevitably led to what we must call by the name of sorcery.

Surrounded as this word is with the odium which credulity on the one hand and imposture on the other have, during many centuries of superstition and ignorance, gradually caused it to be associated, let us consider for a moment its real meaning, and the terrible effects which its practice is ever destined to bring on the world.

Partly through their psychic faculties, which were not yet quenched in the depths of materiality to which the race afterwards descended, and partly through their scientific attainments during this culmination of Atlantean civilization, the most intellec-

tual and energetic members of the race gradually obtained more and more insight into the working of
Nature's laws, and more and more control over
some of her hidden forces. Now the desecration of
this knowledge and its use for selfish ends is what
constitutes sorcery. The awful effects, too, of such
desecration are well enough exemplified in the terrible catastrophes that overtook the race. For when
once the black practice was inaugurated it was destined to spread in ever-widening circles. The higher
spiritual guidance being thus withdrawn, the Kamic
principle, which being the fourth, naturally reached
its zenith during the Fourth Root Race, asserted
itself more and more in humanity. Lust, brutality
and ferocity were all on the increase, and the animal
nature in man was approaching its most degraded
expression. It was a moral question which from the
very earliest times divided the Atlantean Race into
two hostile camps, and what was begun in the
Rmoahal times was terribly accentuated in the Toltec era. The battle of Armageddon is fought over and
over again in every age of the world's history.

No longer submitting to the wise rule of the Initiate emperors, the followers of the ''black arts'' rose
in rebellion and set up a rival emperor, who after
much struggle and fighting drove the white emperor
from his capital, the ''City of the Golden Gates,''
and established himself on his throne.

The white emperor, driven northward, re-estab-
lished himself in a city originally founded by the
Tlavatli on the southern edge of the mountainous
district, but which was now the seat of one of the
tributary Toltec kings. This king gladly welcomed

the white emperor and placed the city at his disposal.
A few more of the tributary kings also remained loyal
to him, but most transferred their allegiance to the
new emperor reigning at the old capital. These, however, did not long remain faithful. Constant asser-
tions of independence were made by the tributary
kings, and continual battles were fought in different
parts of the empire, the practice of sorcery being
largely resorted to, to supplement the powers of
destruction possessed by the armies.

These events took place about 50,000 years before
the first great catastrophe.

From this time onwards things went from bad to
worse. The sorcerers used their powers more and
more recklessly, and greater and greater numbers of
people acquired and practised these terrible "black
arts."

Then came the awful retribution when millions
upon millions perished. The great "City of the
Golden Gates" had by this time become a perfect
den of iniquity. The waves swept over it and
destroyed its inhabitants, and the "black" emperor
and his dynasty fell to rise no more. The emperor of
the north as well as the initiated priests throughout
the whole continent had long been fully aware of the
evil days at hand, and subsequent pages will tell of
the many priest-led emigrations which preceded this
catastrophe, as well as those of later date.

The continent was now terribly rent. But the actual amount of territory submerged by no means represented the damage done, for tidal waves swept over
great tracts of land and left them desolate swamps.
Whole provinces were rendered barren, and re-

mained for generations in an uncultivated and desert condition.

The remaining population too had received a terrible warning. It was taken to heart, and sorcery was for a time less prevalent among them. A long period elapsed before any new powerful rule was established. We shall eventually find a Semite dynasty of sorcerers enthroned in the "City of the Golden Gates," but no Toltec power rose to eminence during the second map period. There were considerable Toltec populations still, but little of the pure blood remained on the mother continent.

On the island of Ruta however, in the third map period, a Toltec dynasty again rose to power and ruled through its tributary kings a large portion of the island. This dynasty was addicted to the black craft, which it must be understood became more and more prevalent during all the four periods, until it culminated in the inevitable catastrophe, which to a great extent purified the earth of the monstrous evil. It must also be borne in mind that down to the very end when Poseidonis disappeared an Initiate emperor or king—or at least one acknowledging the "good law"—held sway in some part of the island continent, acting under the guidance of the Occult Hierarchy in controlling where possible the evil sorcerers, and in guiding and instructing the small minority who were still willing to lead pure and wholesome lives. In later days this "white" king was as a rule elected by the priests—the handful, that is, who still followed the "good law."

Little more remains to be said about the Toltecs. In Poseidonis the population of the whole island was more or less mixed. Two kingdoms and one small republic in the west divided the island between them. The northern portion was ruled by an Initiate king. In the south too the hereditary principle had given way to election by the people. Exclusive race-dynasties were at an end, but kings of Toltec blood occasionally rose to power both in the north and south, the northern kingdom being constantly encroached upon by its southern rival, and more and more of its territory annexed.

Having dealt at some length with the state of things under the Toltecs, the leading political characteristics of the four following sub-races need not long detain us, for none of them reached the heights of civilization that the Toltecs did—in fact the degeneration of the race had set in.

It seems to have been some sort of feudal system that the natural bent of the Turanian race tended to develop. Each chief was supreme on his own territory, and the king was only *primus inter pares*. The chiefs who formed his council occasionally murdered their king and set up one of their own number in his place. They were a turbulent and lawless race—brutal and cruel also. The fact that at some periods of their history regiments of women took part in their wars is significant of the last named characteristics.

But the strange experiment they made in social life which, but for its political origin, would more naturally have been dealt with under "manners and customs," is the most interesting fact in their record. Being continually worsted in war with their Toltec neighbours, knowing themselves to be greatly outnumbered, and desiring above all things increase of population, laws were passed, by which every man was relieved from the direct burden of maintaining his family. The State took charge of and provided for the children, and they were looked upon as its property. This naturally tended to increase the birth-rate amongst the Turanians, and the ceremony of marriage came to be disregarded. The ties of family life, and the feeling of parental love were of course destroyed, and the scheme having been found to be a failure, was ultimately given up. Other attempts at finding socialistic solutions of economical problems which still vex us to-day, were tried and abandoned by this race.

The original Semites, who were a quarrelsome marauding and energetic race, always leant towards a patriarchal form of government. Their colonists, who generally took to the nomadic life, almost exclusively adopted this form, but as we have seen they developed a considerable empire in the days of the second map period, and possessed the great "City of the Golden Gates." They ultimately, however, had to give way before the growing power of the Akkadians.

It was in the third map period, about 100,000 years ago, that the Akkadians finally overthrew the Semite power. The 6th sub-race were a much more law-abiding people than their predecessors. Traders and sailors, they lived in settled communities, and naturally produced an oligarchical form of government. A peculiarity of theirs, of which Sparta is the only modern example, was the dual system of two kings reigning in one city. As a result probably of their sea-going taste, the study of the stars became a characteristic pursuit, and this race made great advances both in astronomy and astrology.

The Mongolian people were an improvement on their immediate ancestors of the brutal Turanian stock. Born as they were on the wide steppes of Eastern Siberia, they never had any touch with the mother-continent, and owing, doubtless, to their environment, they became a nomadic people. More psychic and more religious than the Turanians from whom they sprang, the form of government towards which they gravitated required a suzerain in the background who should be supreme both as a territorial ruler and as a chief high priest.

Emigrations

Three causes contributed to produce emigrations. The Turanian race, as we have seen, was from its very start imbued with the spirit of colonizing, which it carried out on a considerable scale. The Semites and Akkadians were also to a certain extent colonizing races.

Then, as time went on and population tended more and more to outrun the limits of subsistence, necessity operated with the least well-to-do in every race alike, and drove them to seek for a livelihood in less thickly populated countries. For it should be realized that when the Atlanteans reached their zenith in the Toltec era, the proportion of population to the square mile on the continent of Atlantis probably equalled, even if it did not exceed, our modern experience in England and Belgium. It is at all events certain that the vacant spaces available for colonizing were very much larger in that age than in ours, while the total population of the world, which at the present moment is probably not more than twelve hundred to fifteen hundred millions, amounted in those days to the big figure of about two thousand millions.

Lastly, there were the priest-led emigrations which took place prior to each catastrophe—and there were many more of these than the four great ones referred to above. The initiated kings and priests who followed the "good law" were aware beforehand of the impending calamities. Each one, therefore, naturally became a centre of prophetic warning, and ultimately a leader of a band of colonists. It may be noted here that in later days the rulers of the country deeply resented these priest-led emigrations, as tending to impoverish and depopulate their kingdoms, and it became necessary for the emigrants to get on board ship secretly during the night.

In roughly tracing the lines of emigration followed by each sub-race in turn, we shall of necessity ultimately reach the lands which their respective descendants to-day occupy.

For the earliest emigrations we must go back to the Rmoahal days. It will be remembered that that portion of the race which inhabited the northeastern coasts alone retained its purity of blood. Harried on their southern borders and driven further north by the Tlavatli warriors, they began to overflow to the neighbouring land to the east, and to the still nearer promontory of Greenland. In the second map period no pure Rmoahals were left on the then reduced mother-continent but the northern promontory of

the continent then rising on the west was occupied by
them, as well as the Greenland cape already mentioned, and the western shores of the great Scandinavian island. There was also a colony on the land lying north of the central Asian sea.

Brittany and Picardy then formed part of the
Scandinavian island, while the island itself became
in the third map period part of the growing continent
of Europe. Now it is in France that remains of this
race have been found in the quaternary strata, and
the brachycephalous, or round-headed specimen
known as the "Furfooz man," may be taken as a fair
average of the type of the race in its decay.

Many times forced to move south by the rigours of
a glacial epoch, many times driven north by the
greed of their more powerful neighbours, the scattered and degraded remnants of this race may be
found to-day in the modern Lapps, though even here
there was some infusion of other blood. And so it
comes to pass that these faded and stunted specimens
of humanity are the lineal descendants of the black
race of giants who arose on the equatorial lands of
Lemuria well nigh five million years ago.

The Tlavatli colonists seem to have spread out
towards every point of the compass. By the time of
the second map period their descendants were settled
on the western shores of the then growing American
continent (California) as well as on its extreme
southern coasts (Rio de Janeiro). We also find them
occupying the eastern shores of the Scandinavian
island, while numbers of them sailed across the
ocean, rounded the coast of Africa, and reached India. There, mixing with the indigenous Lemurian

population, they formed the Dravidian race. In later days this in its turn received an infusion of Aryan or Fifth Race blood, from which results the complexity of type found in India to-day. In fact we have here a very fair example of the extreme difficulty of deciding any question of race upon merely physical evidence, for it would be quite possible to have Fifth Race egos incarnate among the Brahmans, Fourth Race egos among the lower castes, and some lingering Third Race among the hill tribes.

By the time of the fourth map period we find a Tlavatli people occupying the southern parts of South America, from which it may be inferred that the Patagonians probably had remote Tlavatli ancestry.

Remains of this race, as of the Rmoahals, have been found in the quaternary strata of Central Europe, and the dolichocephalous "Cro-Magnon man"* may be taken as an average specimen of the race in its decadence, while the "Lake-Dwellers" of Switzerland formed an even earlier and not quite pure offshoot. The only people who can be cited as fairly pure-blooded specimens of the race at the present day are some of the brown tribes of Indians of South America. The Burmese and Siamese have also Tlavatli blood in their veins, but in their case it was

---

*Students of geology and palaeontology will know that these sciences regard the "Cro-Magnon man" as prior to the "Furfooz," and seeing that the two races ran alongside each other for vast periods of time, it may quite well be that the individual "Cro-Magnon" skeleton, though representative of the second race, was deposited in the quarternary strata thousands of years before the individual Furfooz man lived on the earth.

mixed with, and therefore dominated by, the nobler stock of one of the Aryan sub-races.

We now come to the Toltecs. It was chiefly to the west that their emigrations tended, and the neighbouring coasts of the American continent were in the second map period peopled by a pure Toltec race, the greater part of those left on the mother-continent being then of very mixed blood. It was on the continents of North and South America that this race spread abroad and flourished, and on which thousands of years later were established the empires of Mexico and Peru. The greatness of these empires is a matter of history, or at least of tradition supplemented by such evidence as is afforded by magnificent architectural remains. It may here be noted that while the Mexican empire was for centuries great and powerful in all that is usually regarded as power and greatness in our civilization of to-day, it never reached the height attained by the Peruvians about 14,000 years ago under their Inca sovereigns, for as regards the general well-being of the people, the justice and beneficence of the government, the equitable nature of the land tenure, and the pure and religious life of the inhabitants, the Peruvian empire of those days might be considered a traditional though faint echo of the golden age of the Toltecs on the mother-continent of Atlantis.

The average Red Indian of North or South America is the best representative to-day of the Toltec people, but of course bears no comparison with the highly civilized individual of the race at its zenith.

First Settlement in Egypt

Egypt must now be referred to, and the consideration of this subject should let in a flood of light upon
its early history. Although the first settlement in that
country was not in the strict sense of the term a colony, it was from the Toltec race that was subsequently drawn the first great body of emigrants intended
to mix with and dominate the aboriginal people.

In the first instance it was the transfer of a great
Lodge of Initiates. This took place about 400,000
years ago. The golden age of the Toltecs was long
past. The first great catastrophe had taken place.
The moral degradation of the people and the consequent practice of the "black arts" were becoming
more accentuated and widely spread. Purer surroundings for the White Lodge were needed. Egypt
was isolated and was thinly peopled, and therefore
Egypt was chosen. The settlement so made answered
its purpose, and undisturbed by adverse conditions
the Lodge of Initiates for nearly 200,000 years did its
work.

About 210,000 years ago, when the time was ripe,
the Occult Lodge founded an empire—the first
"Divine Dynasty" of Egypt—and began to teach the
people. Then it was that the first great body of colonists was brought from Atlantis, and some time
during the ten thousand years that led up to the second catastrophe, the two great Pyramids of Gizeh
were built, partly to provide permanent Halls of Initiation, but also to act as treasure-house and shrine
for some great talisman of power during the submer-

gence which the Initiates knew to be impending. Map No. 3 shows Egypt at that date as under water. It remained so for a considerable period, but on its re-emergence it was again peopled by the descendants of many of its old inhabitants who had retired to the Abyssinian mountains (shown in Map No. 3 as an island) as well as by fresh bands of Atlantean colonists from various parts of the world. A considerable immigration of Akkadians then helped to modify the Egyptian type. This is the era of the second "Divine Dynasty" of Egypt—the rulers of the country being again Initiated Adepts.

The catastrophe of 80,000 years ago again laid the country under water, but this time it was only a temporary wave. When it receded the third "Divine Dynasty"—that mentioned by Manetho—began its rule, and it was under the early kings of this dynasty that the great Temple of Karnak and many of the more ancient buildings still standing in Egypt were constructed. In fact with the exception of the two pyramids no building in Egypt predates the catastrophe of 80,000 years ago.

The final submergence of Poseidonis sent another tidal wave over Egypt. This too, was only a temporary calamity, but it brought the Divine Dynasties to an end, for the Lodge of Initiates had transferred its quarters to other lands.

Various points here left untouched have already been dealt with in the *Transaction of the London Lodge,* "The Pyramids and Stonehenge."

The Turanians who in the first map period had colonized the northern parts of the land lying immediately to the east of Atlantis, occupied in the second map period its southern shores (which included the present Morocco and Algeria). We also find them wandering eastwards, and both the east and west coasts of the central Asian sea were Peopled by them. Bands of them ultimately moved still further east, and the nearest approximation to the type of this race is to-day to be found in the inland Chinese. A curious freak of destiny must be recorded about one of their western offshoots. Dominated all through the centuries by their more powerful Toltec neighbours, it was yet reserved for a small branch of the Turanian stock to conquer and replace the last great empire that the Toltecs raised, for the brutal and barely civilized Aztecs were of pure Turanian blood.

The Semite emigrations were of two kinds, first, those which were controlled by the natural impulse of the race: second, that special emigration which was effected under the direct guidance of the Manu; for, strange as it may seem, it was not from the Toltecs but from this lawless and turbulent, though vigorous and energetic, sub-race that was chosen the nucleus destined to be developed into our great Fifth or Aryan Race. The reason, no doubt, lay in the Mânasic characteristic with which the number five is always associated. The sub-race of that number was inevitably developing its physical brain power and intellect, although at the expense of the psychic perceptions, while that same development of intellect to infinitely higher levels is at once the glory and the destined goal of our Fifth Root Race.

Dealing first with the natural emigrations we find that in the second map period while still leaving powerful nations on the mother continent, the Semites had spread both west and east—west to the lands now forming the United States, and thus accounting for the Semitic type to be found in some of the Indian races, and east to the northern shores of the neighbouring continent, which combined all there then was of Europe, Africa and Asia. The type of the ancient Egyptians, as well as of other neighbouring nations, was to some extent modified by this original Semite blood; but with the exception of the Jews, the only representatives of comparatively unmixed race at the present day are the lighter coloured Kabyles of the Algerian mountain.

The tribes resulting from the segregation effected by the Manu for the formation of the new Root Race eventually found their way to the southern shores of the Central Asian sea, and there the first great Aryan kingdom was established. When the Transaction dealing with the origin of a Root Race comes to be written, it will be seen that many of the peoples we are accustomed to call Semitic are really Aryan in blood. The world will also be enlightened as to what constitutes the claim of the Hebrews to be considered a "chosen people." Shortly it may be stated that they constitute an abnormal and unnatural link between the Fourth and Fifth Root Races.*

The Akkadians, though eventually becoming supreme rulers on the mother continent of Atlantis, owed their birthplace as we have seen in the second map period, to the neighbouring continent—that part occupied by the basin of the Mediterranean

*See W. Williamson's *The Great Law,* pp. 243-5. This statement is the opinion of the author. It is not meant to be derogatory—ED.

about the present island of Sardinia being their special home. From this centre they spread eastwards, occupying what eventually became the shores of the Levant, and reaching as far as Persia and Arabia. As we have seen, they also helped to people Egypt. The early Etruscans, the Phoenicians, including the Carthaginians and the Shumero-Akkads, were branches of this race, while the Basques of to-day have probably more of the Akkadian than of any other blood which flows in their veins.

Stonehenge

A reference to the early inhabitants of our own islands may appropriately be made here, for it was in the early Akkadian days, about 100,000 years ago, that the colony of Initiates who founded Stonehenge landed on these shores—"these shores" being, of course, the shores of the Scandinavian part of the continent of Europe, as shown in Map No. 3. The initiated priests and their followers appear to have belonged to a very early strain of the Akkadian race —they were taller, fairer, and longer headed than the aborigines of the country, who were a very mixed race, but mostly degenerate remnants of the Rmoahals. As readers of the *Transaction of the London Lodge* on the "Pyramids and Stonehenge," will know, the rude simplicity of Stonehenge was intended as a protest against the extravagant ornament and over-decoration of the existing temples in Atlantis, where the debased worship of their own images was being carried on by the inhabitants.

The Mongolians, as we have seen, never had any touch with the mother-continent. Born on the wide plains of Tartary, their emigrations for long found ample scope within those regions; but more than once tribes of Mongol descent have overflowed from northern Asia to America, across Behring's Straits, and the last of such emigrations—that of the Kitans, some 1,300 years ago—has left traces which some western savants have been able to follow. The presence of Mongolian blood in some tribes of North American Indians has also been recognized by various writers on ethnology. The Hungarians and Malays are both known to be offshoots of this race, ennobled in the one case by a strain of Aryan blood, degraded in the other by mixture with the effete Lemurians. But the interesting fact about the Mongolians is that its last family race is still in full force—it has not in fact yet reached its zenith—and the Japanese nation has still got history to give to the world.*

Arts and Sciences

It must primarily be recognized that our own Aryan race has naturally achieved far greater results in almost every direction than did the Atlanteans, but even where they failed to reach our level, the records of what they accomplished are of interest as representing the high water mark which their tide of

---

*Since the above was written the Russo-Japanese war has taken place.

civilization reached. On the other hand, the character of the scientific achievements in which they did
outstrip us are of so dazzling a nature, that bewilder-
ment at such unequal development is apt to be the
feeling left.

The arts and sciences, as practised by the first two
races, were, of course, crude in the extreme, but we
do not propose to follow the progress achieved by
each sub-race separately. The history of the Atlantean, as of the Aryan race, was interspersed with
periods of progress and of decay. Eras of culture
were followed by times of lawlessness, during which
all artistic and scientific development was lost, these
again being succeeded by civilizations reaching to
still higher levels. It must naturally be with the
periods of culture that the following remarks will
deal, chief among which stands out the great Toltec
era.

Architecture and sculpture, painting and music
were all practised in Atlantis. The music even at the
best of times was crude, and the instruments of the
most primitive type. All the Atlantean races were
fond of colour, and brilliant hues decorated both the
insides and the outsides of their houses, but painting
as a fine art was never well established, though in the
later days some kind of drawing and painting was
taught in the schools. Sculpture, on the other hand,
which was also taught in the schools, was widely
practised, and reached great excellence. As we shall
see later on under the head of "Religion" it became
customary for every man who could afford it to place
in one of the temples an image of himself. These
were sometimes carved in wood or in hard black

stone like basalt, but among the wealthy it became the fashion to have their statues cast in one of the precious metals, aurichalcum, gold or silver. A very fair resemblance of the individual usually resulted, while in some cases a striking likeness was achieved.

Architecture

Architecture, however, was naturally the most widely practised of the arts. Their buildings were massive structures of gigantic proportions. The dwelling houses in the cities were not, as ours are, closely crowded together in streets. Like their country houses some stood in their own garden grounds, others were separated by plots of common land, but all were isolated structures. In the case of houses of any importance four blocks of building surrounded a central courtyard, in the centre of which generally stood one of the fountains whose number in the "City of the Golden Gates" gained for it the second appellation of the "City of Waters." There was no exhibition of goods for sale as in modern streets. All transactions of buying and selling took place privately, except at stated times, when large public fairs were held in the open spaces of the cities. But the characteristic feature of the Toltec house was the tower that rose from one of its corners or from the centre of one of the blocks. A spiral staircase built outside led to the upper stories, and a pointed dome terminated the tower—this upper portion being very commonly used as an observatory. As already stated the houses were decorated with bright colours. Some were ornamented with carvings, others with frescoes or painted patterns. The window-spaces were filled with some manufactured article similar to, but less transparent than, glass. The interiors were not furnished with the elaborate detail of our modern dwellings, but the life was highly civilized of its kind.

The temples were huge halls resembling more than anything else the gigantic piles of Egypt, but built on a still more stupendous scale. The pillars supporting the roof were generally square, seldom circular. In the days of the decadence the aisles were surrounded with innumerable chapels in which were enshrined the statues of the more important inhabitants. These side shrines indeed were occasionally of such considerable size as to admit a whole retinue of priests, whom some specially great man might have in his service for the ceremonial worship of his image. Like the private houses the temples too were never complete without the dome-capped towers, which of course were of corresponding size and magnificence. These were used for astronomical observations and for sun-worship.

The precious metals were largely used in the adornment of the temples, the interiors being often not merely inlaid but plated with gold. Gold and silver were highly valued, but as we shall see later on when the subject of the currency is dealt with, the uses to which they were put were entirely artistic and had nothing to do with coinage, while the great quantities that were then produced by the chemists— or as we should now-a-days call them alchemists— may be said to have taken them out of the category of the precious metals. This power of transmutation of

metals was not universal, but it was so widely possessed that enormous quantities were made. In fact
the production of the wished-for metals may be regarded as one of the industrial enterprises of those
days by which these alchemists gained their living.
Gold was admired even more than silver, and was
consequently produced in much greater quantity.

Education

A few words on the subject of language will fitly prelude a consideration of the training in the schools
and colleges of Atlantis. During the first map period
Toltec was the universal language, not only throughout the continent but in the western islands and that
part of the eastern continent which recognized the
emperor's rule. Remains of the Rmoahal and Tlavatli speech survived it is true in out-of-the-way
parts, just as the Celtic and Cymric speech survives
to-day among us in Ireland and Wales. The Tlavatli
tongue was the basis used by the Turanians, who in-
troduced such modifications that an entirely different
language was in time produced; while the Semites
and Akkadians, adopting a Toltec ground-work,
modified it in their respective ways, and so produced
two divergent varieties. Thus in the later days of Poseidonis there were several entirely different languages—all however belonging to the agglutinative
type—for it was not till Fifth Race days that the
descendants of the Semites and Akkadians developed
inflectional speech. All through the ages, however,
the Toltec language fairly maintained its purity, and

the same tongue that was spoken in Atlantis in the days of its splendour was used, with but slight alteration, thousands of years later in Mexico and Peru.

The schools and colleges of Atlantis in the great Toltec days, as well as in subsequent eras of culture, were all endowed by the State. Though every child was required to pass through the primary schools, the subsequent training differed very widely. The primary schools formed a sort of winnowing ground. Those who showed real aptitude for study were, along with the children of the dominant classes who naturally had greater abilities, drafted into the higher schools at about the age of twelve. Reading and writing, which were regarded as mere preliminaries, had already been taught them in the primary schools.

But reading and writing were not considered necessary for the great masses of the inhabitants who had to spend their lives in tilling the land, or in handicrafts, the practice of which was required by the community. The great majority of the children therefore were at once passed on to the technical schools best suited to their various abilities. Chief among these were the agricultural schools. Some branches of mechanics also formed part of the training, while in outlying districts and by the sea-side hunting and fishing were naturally included. And so the children all received the education or training which was most appropriate for them.

The children of superior abilities, who as we have seen had been taught to read and write, had a much more elaborate education. The properties of plants and their healing qualities formed an important branch of study. There were no recognized physicians in those days—every educated man knew more or less of medicine as well as of magnetic healing. Chemistry, mathematics and astronomy were also taught. The training in such studies finds its analogy among ourselves, but the object towards which the teachers' efforts were mainly directed, was the development of the pupil's psychic faculties and his instruction in the more hidden forces of nature. The occult properties of plants, metals, and precious stones, as well as the alchemical processes of transmutation, were included in this category. But as time went on it became more and more the personal power, which Bulwer Lytton calls vril, and the operation of which he has fairly accurately described in his *Coming Race,* that the colleges for the higher training of the youth of Atlantis were specially occupied in developing. The marked change which took place when the decadence of the race set in was, that instead of merit and aptitude being regarded as warrants for advancement to the higher grades of instruction, the dominant classes becoming more and more exclusive allowed none but their own children to graduate in the higher knowledge which gave so much power.

Agriculture

In such an empire as the Toltec, agriculture naturally received much attention. Not only were the labourers taught their duties in technical schools, but colleges were established in which the knowledge necessary for carrying out experiments in the crossing both of animals and plants, was taught to fitting students.

It is said that wheat was not evolved on this planet at all. It was the gift of the Manu who brought it from another globe outside our chain of worlds. But oats and some of our other cereals are the results of crosses between wheat and the wild grasses of the earth. Now the experiments which gave these results were carried out in the agricultural schools of Atlantis. Of course such experiments were guided by high knowledge. But the most notable achievement to be recorded of the Atlantean agriculturists was the evolution of the plantain or banana. In the original wild state it was like an elongated melon with scarcely any pulp, but full of seeds as a melon is. It was of course only by centuries (if not thousands of years) of continuous selection and elimination that the present almost seedless plant was evolved.

Among the domesticated animals of the Toltec days were creatures that looked like very small tapirs. They naturally fed upon roots or herbage, but like the pigs of to-day, which they resembled in more than one particular, they were not over cleanly, and ate whatever came in their way. Large cat-like animals and the wolf-like ancestors of the dog might also be met about human habitations. The Toltec carts appear to have been drawn by creatures somewhat resembling small camels. The Peruvian llamas of to-day are probably their descendants. The ancestors of the Irish elk, too, roamed in herds about the hill sides

in much the same way as our Highland cattle do now
—too wild to allow of easy approach, but still under
the control of man.

Constant experiments were made in breeding and
cross-breeding different kinds of animals, and, curious though it may seem to us, artificial heat was
largely used to force their development, so that the
results of crossing and interbreeding might be more
quickly apparent. The use, too, of different coloured
lights in the chambers where such experiments were
carried on were adopted in order to obtain varying
results.

This control and moulding at will by man of the
animal forms brings us to a rather startling and very
mysterious subject. Reference has been made above
to the work done by the Manus. Now it is in the
mind of the Manu that originates all improvements
in type and the potentialities latent in every form of
being. In order to work out in detail the improvements in the animal forms, the help and co-operation
of man were required. The amphibian and reptile
forms which then abounded had about run their
course, and were ready to assume the more advanced
type of bird or mammal. These forms constituted the
inchoate material placed at man's disposal, and the
clay was ready to assume whatever shape the potter's
hands might mould it into. It was specially with animals in the intermediate stage that so many of the experiments above referred to were tried, and doubtless the domesticated animals like the horse, which
are now of such service to man, are the result of these
experiments in which the men of those days acted in
co-operation with the Manu and his ministers. But

the co-operation was too soon withdrawn. Selfishness obtained the upper hand, and war and discord
brought the Golden Age of the Toltecs to a close.
When instead of working loyally for a common end,
under the guidance of their Initiate kings, men began to prey upon each other, the beasts which might
gradually have assumed, under the care of man,
more and more useful and domesticated forms, being left to the guidance of their own instincts naturally followed the example of their monarch, and began
to prey more and more upon each other. Some indeed had actually already been trained and used by
men in their hunting expeditions, and thus the semi-
domesticated cat-like animals above referred to
naturally became the ancestors of the leopards and
jaguars.

City of the Golden Gates

The "City of the Golden Gates" and its surroundings must be described before we come to consider
the remarkable system by which its inhabitants were
supplied with water. It lay, as we have seen, on the
east coast of the continent close to the sea, and about
15° north of the equator. A beautifully wooded park-
like country surrounded the city. Scattered over a
large area of this were the villa residences of the
wealthier classes. To the west lay a range of mountains, from which the water supply of the city was
drawn. The city itself was built on the slopes of a hill,
which rose from the plain about 500 feet. On the
summit of this hill lay the emperor's palace and gar-

dens, in the centre of which welled up from the earth a neverending stream of water, supplying first the palace and the fountains in the gardens, thence flowing in the four directions and falling in cascades into a canal or moat which encompassed the palace grounds, and thus separated them from the city which lay below on every side. From this canal four channels led the water through four quarters of the city to cascades which in their turn supplied another encircling canal at a lower level. There were three such canals forming concentric circles, the outermost and lowest of which was still above the level of the plain. A fourth canal at this lowest level, but on a rectangular plan, received the constantly flowing waters, and in its turn discharged them into the sea. The city extended over part of the plain, up to the edge of this great outermost moat, which surrounded and defended it with a line of waterways extending about twelve miles by ten miles square.

It will thus be seen that the city was divided into three great belts, each hemmed in by its canals. The characteristic feature of the upper belt that lay just below the palace grounds, was a circular racecourse and large public gardens. Most of the houses of the court officials also lay on this belt, and here also was an institution of which we have no parallel in modern times. The term ''Strangers' Home'' amongst us suggests a mean appearance and sordid surroundings, but this was a palace where all strangers who might come to the city were entertained as long as they might choose to stay—being treated all the time as guests of the Government. The detached houses of the inhabitants and the various temples scattered throughout the city occupied the other two belts. In the days of the Toltec greatness there seems to have been no real poverty—even the retinue of slaves attached to most houses being well fed and clothed —but there were a number of comparatively poor houses in the lowest belt to the north, as well as outside the outermost canal towards the sea. The inhabitants of this part were mostly connected with the shipping, and their houses, though detached, were built closer together than in other districts.

It will be seen from the above that the inhabitants had thus a never-failing supply of pure clear water constantly coursing through the city, while the upper belts and the emperor's palace were protected by lines of moats, each one at a higher level as the centre was approached. It was from a lake which lay among the mountains to the west of the city, at an elevation of about 2,600 feet, that the supply was drawn.

Now it does not require much mechanical knowledge in order to realise how stupendous must have been the works needed to provide this supply, for in the days of its greatness the "City of the Golden Gates" embraced within its four circles of moats over two million inhabitants. No such system of water supply has ever been attempted in Greek, Roman or modern times—indeed it is very doubtful whether our ablest engineers, even at the expenditure of untold wealth, could produce such a result.

Air-Ships

If the system of water supply in the "City of the Golden Gates" was wonderful, the Atlantean methods of locomotion must be recognised as still more marvellous, for the air-ship or flying-machine which Keely in America, and Maxim in this country are now (1895) attempting to produce, was then a realised fact. It was not at any time a common means of transport. The slaves, the servants, and the masses who laboured with their hands, had to trudge along the country tracks, or travel in rude carts with solid wheels drawn by uncouth animals. The air-boats may be considered as the private carriages of those days, or rather the private yachts, if we regard the relative number of those who possessed them, for they must have been at all times difficult and costly to produce. They were not as a rule built to accommodate many persons. Numbers were constructed for only two, some allowed for six or eight passengers. In the later days when war and strife had brought the Golden Age to an end, battle ships that could navigate the air had to a great extent replaced the battle ships at sea—having naturally proved far more powerful engines of destruction. These were constructed to carry as many as fifty, and in some cases even up to a hundred fighting men.

The material of which the air-boats were constructed was either wood or metal. The earlier ones were built of wood—the boards used being exceedingly thin, but the injection of some substance which did not add materially to the weight, while it gave leather-like toughness, provided the necessary combination of lightness and strength. When metal was used it was generally an alloy—two white-coloured metals and one red one entering into its composition. The resultant was white-coloured, like aluminium, and even lighter in weight. Over the rough framework of the air-boat was extended a large sheet of this metal, which was then beaten into shape, and electrically welded where necessary. But whether built of metal or wood their outside surface was apparently seamless and perfectly smooth, and they shone in the dark as if coated with luminous paint.

In shape they were boat-like, but they were invariably decked over, for when at full speed it could not have been convenient, even if safe, for any on board to remain on the upper deck. Their propelling and steering gear could be brought into use at either end.

But the all-interesting question is that relating to the power by which they were propelled. In the earlier times it seems to have been personal vril that supplied the motive power—whether used in conjunction with any mechanical contrivance matters not much—but in the later days this was replaced by a force which, though generated in what is to us an unknown manner, operated nevertheless through definite mechanical arrangements. This force, though not yet discovered by science, more nearly approached that which Keely in America used to handle than the electric power used by Maxim. It was in fact of an etheric nature, but though we are no nearer to the solution of this problem, its method of operation can be described. The mechanical arrangements no doubt differed somewhat in different vessels. The following description is taken from an air-boat in which on one occasion three ambassadors from the king who ruled over the northern part of Poseidonis made the journey to the court of the southern kingdom. A strong heavy metal chest which lay in the centre of the boat was the generator.

Thence the force flowed through two large flexible tubes to either end of the vessel, as well as through eight subsidiary tubes fixed fore and aft to the bulwarks. These had double openings pointing vertically both up and down. When the journey was about to begin the valves of the eight bulwark tubes which pointed downwards were opened—all the other valves being closed. The current rushing through these impinged on the earth with such force as to drive the boat upwards, while the air itself continued to supply the necessary fulcrum. When a sufficient elevation was reached the flexible tube at that end of the vessel which pointed away from the desired destination, was brought into action, while by the partial closing of the valves the current rushing through the eight vertical tubes was reduced to the small amount required to maintain the elevation reached. The great volume of current, being now directed through the large tube pointing downwards from the stern at an angle of about forty-five degrees, while helping to maintain the elevation, provided also the great motive power to propel the vessel through the air. The steering was accomplished by the discharge of the current through this tube, for the slightest change in its direction at once caused an alteration in the vessel's course. But constant supervision was not required. When a long journey had to be taken the tube could be fixed so as to need no handling till the destination was almost reached. The maximum speed attained was about one hundred miles an hour, the course of flight never being a straight line, but always in the form of long waves, now approaching and now receding from the earth.

The elevation at which the vessels travelled was only a few hundred feet—indeed, when high mountains lay in the line of their track it was necessary to change their course and go round them—the more rarefied air no longer supplying the necessary fulcrum. Hills of about one thousand feet were the highest they could cross. The means by which the vessel was brought to a stop on reaching its destination—and this could be done equally well in mid-air —was to give escape to some of the current force through the tube at that end of the boat which pointed towards its destination, and the current impinging on the land or air in front, acted as a drag, while the propelling force behind was gradually reduced by the closing of the valve. The reason has still to be given for the existence of the eight tubes pointing upwards from the bulwarks. This had more especially to do with the aerial warfare. Having so powerful a force at their disposal, the warships naturally directed the current against each other. Now this was apt to destroy the equilibrium of the ship so struck and to turn it upside down—a situation sure to be taken advantage of by the enemy's vessel to make an attack with her ram. There was also the further danger of being precipitated to the ground, unless the shutting and opening of the necessary valves were quickly attended to. In whatever position the vessel might be, the tubes pointing towards the earth were naturally those through which the current should be rushing, while the tubes pointing upwards should be closed. The means by which a vessel turned upside down, might be righted and placed again on a level keel, was accomplished by using the four tubes pointing downwards at one side of the vessel only, while the four at the other side were kept closed.

The Atlanteans had also sea-going vessels which were propelled by some power analogous to that above mentioned, but the current force which was eventually found to be most effective in this case was denser than that used in the air-boats.

Manners and Customs

There was doubtless as much variety in the manners and customs of the Atlanteans at different epochs of their history, as there has been among the various nations which compose our Aryan race. With the fluctuating fashion of the centuries we are not concerned. The following remarks will attempt to deal merely with the leading characteristics which differentiate their habits from our own, and these will be chosen as much as possible from the great Toltec area.

With regard to marriage and the relations of the sexes the experiments made by the Turanians have already been referred to. Polygamous customs were prevalent at different times among all the sub-races, but in the Toltec days while two wives were allowed by the law, great numbers of men had only one wife. Nor were the women—as in countries now-a-days where polygamy prevails—regarded as inferiors, or in the least oppressed. Their position was quite equal to that of the men, while the aptitude many of them displayed in acquiring the vril-power made them fully the equals if not the superiors of the other sex. This equality indeed was recognised from infancy, and there was no separation of the sexes in schools or colleges. Boys and girls were taught together. It was the rule, too, and not the exception, for complete harmony to prevail in the dual households, and the mothers taught their children to look equally to their father's wives for love and protection. Nor were women debarred from taking part in the government. Sometimes they were members of the councils, and occasionally even were chosen by the Adept emperor to represent him in the various provinces as the local sovereigns.

The writing material of the Atlanteans consisted of thin sheets of metal, on the white porcelain-like surface of which the words were written. They also had the means of reproducing the written text by placing on the inscribed sheet another thin metal plate which had previously been dipped in some liquid. The text thus graven on the second plate could be reproduced at will on other sheets, a great number of which fastened together constituted a book.

Food

A custom which differs considerably from our own must be instanced next, in their choice of food. It is an unpleasant subject, but can scarcely be passed over. The flesh of the animals they usually discarded, while the parts which among us are avoided as food, were by them devoured. The blood also they drank—often hot from the animal—and various cooked dishes were also made of it.

It must not, however, be thought that they were without the lighter, and to us, more palatable, kinds of food. The seas and rivers provided them with fish, the flesh of which they ate, though often in such an advanced stage of decomposition as would be to us revolting. The different grains were largely cultivated, of which were made bread and cakes. They also had milk, fruit and vegetables.

A small minority of the inhabitants, it is true, never adopted the revolting customs above referred to. This was the case with the Adept kings and emperors and the initiated priesthood throughout the whole empire. They were entirely vegetarian in their habits, but though many of the emperor's counsellors and the officials about the court affected to prefer the purer diet, they often indulged in secret their grosser tastes.

Nor were strong drinks unknown in those days. Fermented liquor of a very potent sort was at one time much in vogue. But it was so apt to make those who drank it dangerously excited that a law was passed absolutely forbidding its consumption.

Weapons

The weapons of warfare and the chase differed considerably at different epochs. Swords and spears, bows and arrows sufficed as a rule for the Rmoahals and the Tlavatli. The beasts which they hunted at that very early period were mammoths with long woolly hair, elephants and hippopotami. Marsupials also abounded as well as survivals of intermediate types—some being half reptile and half mammal, others half reptile and half bird.

The use of explosives was adopted at an early period, and carried to great perfection in later times. Some appear to have been made to explode on concussion, others after a certain interval of time, but in either case the destruction to life seems to have resulted from the release of some poisonous vapour, not from the impact of bullets. So powerful indeed must have become these explosives in later Atlantean times, that we hear of whole companies of men being destroyed in battle by the noxious gas generated by the explosion of one of these bombs above their heads, thrown there by some sort of lever.

Money

The monetary system must now be considered. During the first three sub-races at all events, such a thing as a State coinage was unknown. Small pieces of metal or leather stamped with some given value were, it is true, used as tokens. Having a perforation in the centre they were strung together, and were usually carried at the girdle. But each man was, as it were, his own coiner, and the leather or metal token fabricated by him and exchanged with another for value received, was but a personal acknowledgment of indebtedness, such as a promissory note is among us. No man was entitled to fabricate more of these tokens than he was able to redeem by the transfer of goods in his possession. The tokens did not circulate as coinage does, while the holder of the token had the means to estimate with perfect accuracy the resources of his debtor by the clairvoyant faculty which all then possessed to a greater or less degree, and which in any case of doubt was instantly directed to ascertain the actual state of the facts.

It must be stated, however, that in the later days of Poseidonis, a system approximating to our own currency was adopted, and the triple mountain visible from the great southern capital was the favourite representation on the State coinage.

Land Tenure

But the system of land tenure is the most important subject under this heading. Among the Rmoahal and Tlavatli, who lived chiefly by hunting and fishing, the question naturally did not arise, though some system of village cultivation was recognized in the Tlavatli days.

It was with the increase of population and civilization in the early Toltec times that land first became worth fighting for. It is not proposed to trace the system or want of system prevalent in the troublous times anterior to the advent of the Golden Age. But the records of that epoch present to the consideration, not only of political economists, but of all who regard the welfare of the race, subject of the utmost interest and importance.

The population, it must be remembered, had been

steadily increasing, and under the government of the Adept emperors it had reached the very large figure already quoted; nevertheless poverty and want were things undreamt of in those days, and this social well-being was no doubt partly due to the system of land tenure.

Not only was all the land and its produce regarded as belonging to the emperor, but all the flocks and herds upon it were his as well. The country was divided into different provinces or districts, each province having at its head one of the subsidiary kings or viceroys appointed by the emperor. Each of these viceroys was held responsible for the government and well-being of all the inhabitants under his rule. The tillage of the land, the harvesting of the crops, and the pasturage of the herds lay within his sphere of superintendence as well as the conducting of such agricultural experiments as have been already referred to.

Each viceroy had round him a council of agricultural advisers and coadjutors, who had amongst their other duties to be well versed in astronomy, for it was not a barren science in those days. The occult influences on plant and animal life were then studied and taken advantage of. The power, too, of producing rain at will was not uncommon then, while the effects of a glacial epoch were on more than one occasion partly neutralized in the northern parts of the continent by occult science. The right day for beginning every agricultural operation was of course duly calculated, and the work carried into effect by the officials whose duty it was to supervise every detail. The produce raised in each district or kingdom was as a rule consumed in it, but an exchange of agricultural commodities was sometimes arranged between the rulers.

After a small share had been put aside for the emperor and the central government at the "City of the Golden Gates," the produce of the whole district or kingdom was divided among the inhabitants—the local viceroy and his retinue of officials naturally receiving the larger portions, but the meanest agricultural labourer getting enough to secure him competence and comfort. Any increase in the productive capacity of the land, or in the mineral wealth which it yielded, was divided proportionately amongst all concerned—all, therefore, were interested in making the result of their combined labour as lucrative as possible.

This system worked admirably for a very long period. But as time went on negligence and self-seeking crept in. Those whose duty it was to superintend, threw more and more responsibility on their inferiors in office, and in time it became rare for the rulers to interfere or to interest themselves in any of the operations. This was the beginning of the evil days. The members of the dominant class who had previously given all their time to the state duties began to think about making their own lives more pleasant. The elaboration of luxury was setting in.

There was one cause in particular which produced great discontent amongst the lower classes. The system under which the youth of the nation was drafted into the technical schools has already been referred to. Now it was always one of the superior class whose psychic faculties had been duly cultivated, to whom the duty was assigned of selecting the children so that each one should receive the training, and ultimately be devoted to the occupation, for which he was naturally most fitted. But when those possessed of the clairvoyant vision, by which alone such choice could be made, delegated their duties to inferiors who were wanting in such psychic attributes, the results ensuing were that the children were often thrust into wrong grooves, and those whose capacity and taste lay in one direction often found themselves tied for life to an occupation which they disliked, and in which, therefore, they were rarely successful.

The systems of land tenure which ensued in different parts of the empire on the breaking up of the great Toltec dynasty were many and various. But it is not necessary to follow them. In the later days of Poseidonis they had, as a rule, given place to the system of individual ownership which we know so well.

Reference has already been made, under the head of ''Emigrations,'' to the system of land tenure which prevailed during that glorious period of Peruvian history when the Incas held sway about 14,000 years ago. A short summary of this may be of interest as demonstrating the source from which its groundwork was doubtless derived, as well as instancing the variations which had been adopted in this somewhat more complicated system.

All title to land was derived in the first instance from the Inca, but half of it was assigned to the cultivators, who of course constituted the great bulk of the population. The other half was divided between the Inca and the priesthood who celebrated the worship of the sun.

Out of the proceeds of his specially allotted lands the Inca had to keep up the army, the roads throughout the whole empire, and all the machinery of government. This was conducted by a special governing class, all more or less closely related to the Inca himself, and representing a civilization and a culture much in advance of the great masses of the population.

The remaining fourth—"the lands of the sun"— provided not only for the priests who conducted the public worship throughout the empire, but for the entire education of the people in schools and colleges, for all sick and infirm persons, and finally, for every inhabitant (exclusive, of course, of the governing class for whom there was no cessation of work) on reaching the age of forty-five, that being the age arranged for the hard work of life to cease, and for leisure and enjoyment to begin.

Religion

The only subject that now remains to be dealt with is the evolution of religious ideas. Between the spiritual aspiration of a rude but simple race and the degraded ritual of an intellectually cultured but spiritually dead people, lies a gulf which only the term religion, used in its widest acceptation, can span. Nevertheless, it is this consecutive process of generation and degeneration which has to be traced in the history of the Atlantean people.

It will be remembered that the government under which the Rmoahals came into existence, was described as the most perfect conceivable, for it was the Manu himself who acted as their king. The memory of this divine ruler was naturally preserved in the annals of the race, and in due time he came to be regarded as a god, among a people who were naturally psychic, and had consequently glimpses of those states of consciousness which transcend our ordinary waking condition. Retaining these higher attributes it was only natural that this primitive people should adopt a religion which, though in no way representative of any exalted philosophy, was of a type far from ignoble. In later days this phase of religious belief passed into a kind of ancestor-worship.

The Tlavatli, while inheriting the traditional reverence and worship for the Manu, were taught by Adept instructors of the existence of a Supreme Being whose symbol was recognised as the sun. They thus developed a sort of sun worship, for the practice of which they repaired to the hill-tops. There they built great circles of upright monoliths. These were intended to be symbolical of the sun's yearly course, but they were also used for astronomical purposes—being placed so that, to one standing at the high altar, the sun would rise at the winter solstice behind one of these monoliths, at the vernal equinox behind another, and so on throughout the year. Astronomical observations of a still more complex character connected with the more distant constellations were also helped by these stone circles.

We have already seen under the head of emigrations how a later sub-race—the Akkadians—in the

erection of Stonehenge, reverted to this primitive
building of monoliths.

Endowed though the Tlavatli were with somewhat
greater capacity for intellectual development than
the previous sub-race, their cult was still of a very
primitive type.

With the wider diffusion of knowledge in the days
of the Toltecs, and more especially with the estab-
lishment later on of an initiated priesthood and an
Adept emperor, increased opportunities were offered
to the people for the attainment of a truer conception
of the divine. The few who were ready to take full advantage of the teaching offered, after having been
tried and tested, were doubtless admitted into the
ranks of the priesthood, which then constituted an
immense occult fraternity. With these, however,
who had so outstripped the mass of humanity, as to
be ready to begin the progress of the occult path, we
are not here concerned, the religions practised by the
inhabitants of Atlantis generally being the subject of
our investigation.

The power to rise to philosophic heights of thought
was of course wanting to the masses of those days, as
it is similarly wanting to the great majority of the inhabitants of the world to-day. The nearest approach
which the most gifted teacher could make in attempting to convey any idea of the nameless and all-per-
vading essence of the Cosmos was necessarily imparted in the form of symbols, and the sun naturally
enough was the first symbol adopted. As in our own
days too, the more cultivated and spiritually-minded
would see through the symbol, and might sometimes

rise on the wings of devotion to the Father of our spirits, that

''Motive and centre of our soul's desire,

Object and refuge of our journey's end,''

while the grosser multitude would see nothing but the symbol, and would worship it, as the carved Madonna or the wooden image of the Crucified One is to-day worshipped throughout Catholic Europe.

Sun and fire worship then became the cult for the celebration of which magnificent temples were reared throughout the length and breadth of the continent of Atlantis, but more especially in the great ''City of the Golden Gates''—the temple-service being performed by retinues of priests endowed by the State for that purpose.

In those early days no image of the Deity was permitted. The sun-disk was considered the only appropriate emblem of the godhead, and as such was used in every temple, a golden disk being generally placed so as to catch the first rays of the rising sun at the vernal equinox or at the summer solstice.

An interesting example of the almost unalloyed survival of this worship of the sun-disk may be instanced in the Shinto ceremonies of Japan. All other representation of Deity is, in this faith, regarded as impious, and even the circular mirror of polished metal is hidden from the vulgar gaze save on ceremonial occasions. Unlike the gorgeous temple decorations of Atlantis, however, the Shinto temples are characterized by an entire absence of decoration—the exquisite finish of the plain wood-work being unrelieved by any carving, paint or varnish.

But the sun-disk did not always remain the only permissible emblem of Deity. The image of a man— an archetypal man—was in after days placed in the temples and adored as the highest representation of the divine. In some ways this might be considered a reversion to the Rmoahal worship of the Manu. Even then the religion was comparatively pure, and the occult fraternity of the ''Good Law'' of course did their utmost to keep alive in the hearts of the people the spiritual life.

The evil days, however, were drawing near when no altruistic idea should remain to redeem the race from the abyss of selfishness in which it was destined to be overwhelmed. The decay of the ethical idea was the necessary prelude to the perversion of the spiritual. The hand of every man fought for himself alone, and his knowledge was used for purely selfish ends, till it became an established belief that there was nothing in the universe greater or higher than themselves. Each man was his own ''Law, and Lord and God,'' and the very worship of the temples ceased to be the worship of any ideal, but became the mere adoration of man as he was known and seen to be. As is written in the *Book of Dzyan,* ''Then the Fourth became tall with pride. We are the kings it was said; we are the Gods. . . . They built huge cities. Of rare earths and metals they built, and out of the fires vomited, out of the white stone of the mountains and of the black stone, they cut their own images in their size and likeness, and worshipped them.'' Shrines were placed in temples in which the statue of each man, wrought in gold or silver, or carved in stone or wood, was adored by himself. The richer men kept whole trains of priests in their employ for the cult and care of their shrines, and offerings were made to these statues as to gods. The apotheosis of self could go no further.

It must be remembered that every true religious idea that has ever entered into the mind of man, has been consciously suggested to him by the divine Instructors or the Initiates of the White Lodge, who throughout all the ages have been the guardians of the divine mysteries, and of the facts of the supersensual states of consciousness.

Mankind generally has but slowly become capable of assimilating a few of these divine ideas, while the monstrous growths and hideous distortions to which every religion on earth stands as witness, must be traced to man's own lower nature. It would seem indeed that he has not always even been fit to be entrusted with knowledge as to the mere symbols under which were veiled the light of Deity, for in the days of the Turanian Supremacy some of this knowledge was wrongfully divulged.

We have seen how the life and light giving attributes of the sun were in early times used as the symbol to bring before the minds of the people all that they were capable of conceiving of the great First Cause. But other symbols of far deeper and more real significance were known and guarded within the ranks of the priesthood. One of these was the conception of a Trinity in Unity. The Trinities of most sacred significance were never divulged to the people, but the Trinity personifying the cosmic powers of the universe as Creator, Preserver, and Destroyer, became publicly known in some irregular manner in the Turanian days. This idea was still further materialized and degraded by the Semites into a strictly anthropomorphic Trinity consisting of father, mother and child.

A further and rather terrible development of the Turanian times must still be referred to. With the practice of sorcery many of the inhabitants had, of course, become aware of the existence of powerful elementals—creatures who had been called into being, or at least animated by their own powerful wills, which being directed towards maleficent ends, naturally produced elementals of power and malignity. So degraded had then become man's feelings of reverence and worship, that they actually began to adore these semi-conscious creations of their own malignant thought. The ritual with which these beings were worshipped was bloodstained from the very start, and of course every sacrifice offered at their shrines gave vitality and persistence to these vampire-like creations—so much so, that even to the present day in various parts of the world, the elementals formed by the powerful will of these old Atlantean sorcerers still continue to exact their tribute from unoffending village communities.

Though inaugurated and widely practised by the brutal Turanians, this blood-stained ritual seems never to have spread to any extent among the other sub-races, though human sacrifices appear to have been not uncommon among some branches of the Semites.

In the great Toltec empire of Mexico the sun-worship of their forefathers was still the national religion, while the bloodless offerings to their benefi- cent Deity, Quetzalcoatl, consisted merely of flowers and fruit. It was only with the coming of the savage Aztecs that the harmless Mexican ritual was supple- mented with the blood of human sacrifices, which drenched the altars of their war-god, Huitzilopo- chtli, and the tearing out of the hearts of the victims on the summit of the Teocali may be regarded as a direct survival of the elemental-worship of their Turanian ancestors in Atlantis.

It will be seen then that as in our own days, the re- ligious life of the people embraced the most varied forms of belief and worship. From the small minority who aspired to initiation, and had touch with the higher spiritual life—who knew that good will to- wards all men, control of thought, and purity of life and action were the necessary preliminaries to the at- tainment of the highest states of consciousness and the widest realms of vision—innumerable phases led down through the more or less blind worship of cos- mic powers, or of anthropomorphic gods, to the de- graded but most widely extended ritual in which each man adored his own image, and to the blood stained rites of the elemental worship.

It must be remembered throughout that we are dealing with the Atlantean race only, so that any ref- erence would be out of place that bore on the still more degraded fetish-worship that even then existed —as it still does—amongst the debased representa- tives of the Lemurian peoples.

All through the centuries then, the various rituals composed to celebrate these various forms of worship

were carried on, till the final submergence of Poseidonis, by which time the countless hosts of Atlantean
emigrants had already established on foreign lands
the various cults of the mother-continent.

To trace the rise and follow the progress in detail
of the archaic religions, which in historic times have
blossomed into such diverse and antagonistic forms,
would be an undertaking of great difficulty, but the
illumination it would throw on matters of transcendent importance may some day induce the attempt.

In conclusion, it would be vain to attempt to summarize what is already too much of a summary.
Rather let us hope that the foregoing may lend itself
as the text from which may be developed histories of
the many offshoots of the various sub-races—histories which may analytically examine political and
social developments which have been here touched
on in the most fragmentary manner.

One word, however, may still be said about that
evolution of the race—that progress which all creation, with mankind at its head, is ever destined to
achieve century by century, millennium by millennium, manvantara by manvantara, and kalpa by
kalpa.

The descent of spirit into matter—those two poles
of the one eternal substance—is the process which
occupies the first half of every cycle. Now the period
we have been contemplating in the foregoing pages
—the period during which the Atlantean race was
running its course—was the very middle or turning
point of this present manvantara.

The process of evolution which in our present
Fifth Race has now set in—the return, that is, of

matter into spirit—had in those days revealed itself in but a few isolated individual cases—forerunners of the resurrection of the spirit.

But the problem, which all who have given the subject any amount of consideration must have felt to be still awaiting a solution, is the surprising contrast in the attributes of the Atlantean race. Side by side with their brutal passions, their degraded animal propensities, were their psychic faculties, their godlike intuition.

Now the solution of this apparently insoluble enigma lies in the fact that the building of the bridge had only then been begun—the bridge of Manas, or mind, destined to unite in the perfected individual the upward surging forces of the animal and the downward cycling spirit of the God. The animal kingdom of to-day exhibits a field of nature where the building of that bridge has not yet been begun, and even among mankind in the days of Atlantis the connection was so slight that the spiritual attributes had but little controlling power over the lower animal nature. The touch of mind they had was sufficient to add zest to the gratification of the senses, but was not enough to vitalize the still dormant spiritual faculties, which in the perfected individual will have to become the absolute monarch. Our metaphor of the bridge may carry us a little further if we consider it as now in process of construction, but as destined to remain incomplete for mankind in general for untold millenniums—in fact, until Humanity has completed another circle of the seven planets and the great Fifth Round is half way through its course.

Though it was during the latter half of the Third

Root Race and the beginning of the Fourth that the Manasaputra descended to endow with mind the bulk of Humanity who were still without the spark, yet so feebly burned the light all through the Atlantean days that few could be said to have attained to the powers of abstract thought. On the other hand, the functioning of the mind on concrete things came well within their grasp, and as we have seen it was in the practical concerns of their every-day life, especially when their psychic faculties were directed towards the same objects, that they achieved such remarkable and stupendous results.

It must also be remembered that Kama, the fourth principle, naturally obtained its culminating development in the Fourth Race. This would account for the depths of animal grossness to which they sank, whilst the approach of the cycle to its nadir inevitably accentuated this downward movement, so that there is little to be surprised at in the gradual loss by the race of the psychic faculties, and in its descent to selfishness and materialism.

Rather should all this be regarded as part of the great cyclic process in obedience to the eternal law.

We have all gone through those evil days, and the experiences we then accumulated go to make up the characters we now possess.

But a brighter sun now shines on the Aryan race than that which lit the path of their Atlantean forefathers. Less dominated by the passions of the senses, more open to the influence of mind, the men of our race have obtained and are obtaining a firmer grasp of knowledge, a wider range of intellect. This upward arc of the great manvantaric cycle will naturally lead increasing numbers towards the entrance of the Path, and will lend more and more attraction to the transcendent opportunities it offers for the continued strengthening and purification of the character—strengthening and purification no longer directed by mere spasmodic effort, and continually interrupted by misleading attractions, but guided and guarded at every step by the Masters of Wisdom, so that the upward climb when once begun should no longer be halting and uncertain, but lead direct to the glorious goal.

The psychic faculties too, and the godlike intuition, lost for a time but still the rightful heritage of the race, only await the individual effort of reattainment, to give to the character still deeper insight and more transcendent powers. So shall the ranks of the Adept instructors—the Masters of Wisdom—be ever strengthened and recruited, and even amongst us today there must certainly be some, indistinguishable save by the deathless enthusiasm with which they are animated, who will, before the next Root Race is established on this planet, stand themselves as Masters of Wisdom to help the race in its upward progress.

The Lost Lemuria

Foreword

The object of this paper is not so much to bring forward startling information about the lost continent of Lemuria and its inhabitants, as to establish by the evidence obtainable from geology and from the study of the relative distribution of living and extinct animals and plants, as well as from the observed processes of physical evolution in the lower kingdoms, the facts stated in *The Secret Doctrine* and in other works with reference to these now submerged lands.

IT IS GENERALLY recognised by science that what is now dry land, on the surface of our globe, was once the ocean floor, and that what is now the ocean floor was once dry land. Geologists have in some cases been able to specify the exact portions of the earth's surface where these subsidences and up-heavals have taken place, and although the lost continent of Atlantis has so far received scant recognition from the world of science, the general concensus of opinion has for long pointed to the existence, at some prehistoric time, of a vast southern continent to which the name of Lemuria has been assigned.

Evidence supplied by Geology and by the relative distribution of living and extinct Animals and Plants

"The history of the earth's development shows us that the distribution of land and water on its surface is ever and continually changing. In consequence of geological changes of the earth's crust, *elevations* and *depressions* of the ground take place everywhere, sometimes more strongly marked in one place, sometimes in another. Even if they happen so slowly that in the course of centuries the seashore rises or sinks only a few inches, or even only a few lines, still they nevertheless effect great results in the course of

long periods of time. And long—immeasurably long
—periods of time have not been wanting in the
earth's history. During the course of many millions
of years, ever since organic life existed on the earth,
land and water have perpetually struggled for supremacy. Continents and islands have sunk into the
sea, and new ones have arisen out of its bosom.
Lakes and seas have been slowly raised and dried
up, and new water basins have arisen by the sinking
of the ground. Peninsulas have become islands by
the narrow neck of land which connected them with
the mainland sinking into the water. The islands of
an archipelago have become the peaks of a continuous chain of mountains by the whole floor of their
sea being considerably raised.

"Thus the Mediterranean at one time was an inland sea, when in the place of the Straits of Gibraltar, an isthmus connected Africa with Spain. England even during the more recent history of the
earth, when man already existed, has repeatedly
been connected with the European continent and
been repeatedly separated from it. Nay, even Europe and North America have been directly connected. The South Sea at one time formed a large
Pacific Continent, and the numerous little islands
which now lie scattered in it were simply the highest
peaks of the mountains covering that continent. The
Indian Ocean formed a continent which extended
from the Sunda Islands along the southern coast of
Asia to the east coast of Africa. This large continent
of former times Sclater, an Englishman, has called
Lemuria, from the monkey-like animals which inhabited it, and it is at the same time of great importance from being the probable cradle of the human

race, which in all likelihood here first developed out of anthropoid apes.* The important proof which Alfred Wallace has furnished, by the help of chorological facts, that the present Malayan Archipelago consists in reality of two completely different divisions, is particularly interesting. The western division, the Indo-Malayan Archipelago, comprising the large islands of Borneo, Java and Sumatra, was formerly connected by Malacca with the Asiatic continent, and probably also with the Lemurian continent just mentioned. The eastern division on the other hand, the Austro-Malayan Archipelago, comprising Celebes, the Moluccas, New Guinea, Solomon's Islands, etc., was formerly directly connected with Australia. Both divisions were formerly two continents separated by a strait, but they have now for the most part sunk below the level of the sea. Wallace, solely on the ground of his accurate chorological observations, has been able in the most accurate manner to determine the position of this former strait, the south end of which passes between Balij and Lombok.

"Thus, ever since liquid water existed on the earth, the boundaries of water and land have eternally changed, and we may assert that the outlines of continents and islands have never remained for an hour, nay, even for a minute, exactly the same. For the waves eternally and perpetually break on the edge of the coast, and whatever the land in these

---

*Haeckel is correct enough in his surmise that Lemuria was the cradle of the human race as it now exists, but it was not out of Anthropoid apes that mankind developed. A reference will be made later on to the position in nature which the Anthropoid apes really occupy.

places loses in extent, it gains in other places by the accumulation of mud, which condenses into solid stone and again rises above the level of the sea as new land. Nothing can be more erroneous than the idea of a firm and unchangeable outline of our continents, such as is impressed upon us in early youth by defective lessons on geography, which are devoid of a geological basis.''*

The name Lemuria, as above stated, was originally adopted by Mr. Sclater in recognition of the fact that it was probably on this continent that animals of the Lemuroid type were developed.

''This,'' writes A. R. Wallace, ''is undoubtedly a legitimate and highly probable supposition, and it is an example of the way in which a study of the geographical distribution of animals may enable us to reconstruct the geography of a bygone age. . . . It [this continent] represents what was probably a primary zoological region in some past geological epoch; but what that epoch was and what were the limits of the region in question, we are quite unable to say. If we are to suppose that it comprised the whole area now inhabited by Lemuroid animals, we must make it extend from West Africa to Burmah, South China and Celebes, an area which it possibly did once occupy.''†

*Ernst Haeckel's ''Hist. of Creation,'' 2nd ed., 1876, Vol. I., pp. 360-62.

†Alfred Russell Wallace's ''The Geographical Distribution of Animals—with a study of the relations of living and extinct Faunas as elucidating the past changes of the Earth's Surface.'' London: Macmillan & Co., 1876. Vol. I., pp. 76-7.

"We have already had occasion," he elsewhere writes, "to refer to an ancient connection between this sub-region (the Ethiopian) and Madagascar, in order to explain the distribution of the Lemurine type, and some other curious affinities between the two countries. This view is supported by the geology of India, which shows us Ceylon and South India consisting mainly of granite and old-metamorphic rocks, while the greater part of the peninsula is of tertiary formation, with a few isolated patches of secondary rocks. It is evident, therefore, that during much of the tertiary period,* Ceylon and South India were bounded on the north by a considerable extent of sea, and probably formed part of an extensive Southern Continent or great island. The very numerous and remarkable cases of affinity with Malaya, require, however, some closer approximation with these islands, which probably occurred at a later period. When, still later, the great plains and tablelands of Hindostan were formed, and a permanent land communication effected with the rich and highly developed Himalo-Chinese fauna, a rapid immigration of new types took place, and many of the less specialised forms of mammalia and birds became extinct. Among reptiles and insects the competition was less severe, or the older forms were too well adapted to local conditions to be expelled; so that it is among these groups alone that we find any considerable number of what are probably the

*Ceylon and South India, it is true, have been bounded on the north by a considerable extent of sea, but that was at a much earlier date than the Tertiary period.

remains of the ancient fauna of a now submerged Southern Continent."*

After stating that during the whole of the tertiary and perhaps during much of the secondary periods, the great land masses of the earth were probably situated in the Northern Hemisphere, Wallace proceeds, "In the Southern Hemisphere there appear to have been three considerable and very ancient land masses, varying in extent from time to time, but always keeping distinct from each other, and represented more or less completely by Australia, South Africa and South America of our time. Into these flowed successive waves of life as they each in turn became temporarily united with some part of the Northern land."†

Although, apparently in vindication of some conclusions of his which had been criticised by Dr. Hartlaub, Wallace subsequently denied the necessity of postulating the existence of such a continent, his general recognition of the facts of subsidences and upheavals of great portions of the earth's surface, as well as the inferences which he draws from the acknowledged relations of living and extinct faunas as above stated, remain of course unaltered.

The following extracts from Mr. H. F. Blandford's most interesting paper read before a meeting of the Geological Society deals with the subject in still greater detail‡:—

*Wallace's "Geographical Distribution, etc.," Vol. I., pp. 328-9.
†Wallace's "Geographical Distribution, etc.," Vol. II., p. 155.
‡H. F. Blandford "On the age and correlations of the Plant-bearing series of India and the former existence of an Indo-

"The affinities between the fossils of both animals and plants of the Beaufort group of Africa and those of the Indian Panchets and Kathmis are such as to suggest the former existence of a land connexion between the two areas. But the resemblance of the African and Indian fossil faunas does not cease with Permian and Triassic times. The plant beds of the Uitenhage group have furnished eleven forms of plants, two of which Mr. Tate has identified with Indian Rájmahál plants. The Indian Jurassic fossils have yet to be described (with a few exceptions), but it has been stated that Dr. Stoliezka was much struck with the affinities of certain of the Cutch fossils to African forms; and Dr. Stoliezka and Mr. Griesbach have shown that of the Cretaceous fossils of the Umtafuni river in Natal, the majority (22 out of 35 described forms) are identical with species from Southern India. Now the plant-bearing series of India and the Karoo and part of the Uitenhage formation of Africa are in all probability of fresh-water origin, both indicating the existence of a large land area around, from the waste of which these deposits are derived. Was this land continuous between the two regions? And is there anything in the present physical geography of the Indian Ocean which would suggest its probable position? Further, what was the connexion between this land and Australia which we must equally assume to have existed in Permian times? And, lastly, are there any peculiarities in the existing fauna and flora of India, Africa and the intervening islands which would lend support to the idea of a former connexion more direct than that which now exists between Africa and South India and the Malay peninsula? The speculation here put forward is no new one. It has long been a subject of thought in the minds of some Indian and European naturalists, among the former of whom I may mention my brother [Mr. Blandford] and Dr. Stoliezka, their speculations being grounded on the relationship and partial identity of the faunas and floras of past times, not less than on that existing community of forms which has led Mr. Andrew Murray, Mr. Searles, V. Wood, jun., and Professor Huxley to infer the existence of a Miocene continent occupying a part of the Indian Ocean. Indeed, all that I can pretend to aim at in this paper is to endeavour to give some additional definition and extension to the conception of its geological aspect.

"With regard to the geographical evidence, a glance at the map will show that from the neighbourhood of the West Coast of India to that of the Seychelles, Madagascar, and the Mauritius, extends a line of coral atolls and banks, including Adas bank, the Laccadives, Maldives, the Chagos group and the Saya de Mulha, all indicating the existence of a submerged mountain range or ranges. The Seychelles, too, are mentioned by Mr. Darwin as rising from an extensive and tolerably level bank having a depth of between 30 and 40 fathoms; so that, although now partly encircled by fringing reefs, they may be regarded as a virtual extension of the same submerged axis. Further west the Cosmoledo and Comoro Islands consist of atolls and islands surrounded

by barrier reefs; and these bring us pretty close to the present shores of Africa and Madagascar. It seems at least probable that in this chain of atolls, banks, and barrier reefs we have indicated the position of an ancient mountain chain, which possibly formed the back-bone of a tract of later Palaeozoic Mesozoic, and early Tertiary land, being related to it much as the Alpine and Himálayan system is to the Europaeo-Asiatic continent, and the Rocky Mountains and Andes to the two Americas. As it is desirable to designate this Mesozoic land by a name, I would propose that of Indo-Oceana. [The name given to it by Mr. Sclater, *viz.*, Lemuria, is, however, the one which has been most generally adopted.] Professor Huxley has suggested on palaeontological grounds that a land connexion existed in this region (or rather between Abyssinia and India) during the Miocene epoch. From what has been said above it will be seen that I infer its existence from a far earlier date.*
With regard to its depression, the only present evidence relates to its northern extremity, and shows that it was in this region, later than the great trap-flows of the Dakhan. These enormous sheets of volcanic rock are remarkably horizontal to the east of the Gháts and the Sakyádri range, but to the west of this they begin to dip seawards, so that the island of Bombay is composed of the higher parts of the formation. This indicates only that the depression to the westward has taken place in Tertiary times; and to

*A reference to the maps will show that Mr. Blandford's estimate of date is the more correct of the two.

that extent Professor Huxley's inference, that it was after the Miocene period, is quite consistent with the geological evidence.''

After proceeding at some length to instance the close relationship of many of the fauna in the lands under consideration (Lion, Hyaena, Jackal, Leopard, Antelope, Gazelle, Sand-grouse, Indian Bustard, many Land Molusca, and notably the Lemur and the Scaly Anteater) the writer proceeds as follows: —

''Palaeontology, physical geography and geology, equally with the ascertained distribution of living animals and plants, offer thus their concurrent testimony to the former close connexion of Africa and India, including the tropical islands of the Indian Ocean. This Indo-Oceanic land appears to have existed from at least early Permian times, probably (as Professor Huxley has pointed out) up to the close of the Miocene epoch;* and South Africa and Peninsular India are the existing remnants of that ancient land. It may not have been absolutely continuous during the whole of this long period. Indeed, the Cretaceous rocks of Southern India and Southern Africa, and the marine Jurassic beds of the same regions, prove that some portions of it were, for longer or shorter periods, invaded by the sea; but any break of continuity was probably not prolonged; for Mr. Wallace's investigations in the Eastern Archipelago have shown how narrow a sea may offer an insuperable barrier to the migration of land animals. In Pa-

*Parts of the continent of course endured, but the dismemberment of Lemuria is said to have taken place before the beginning of the Eocene Age.

laeozoic times this land must have been connected
with Australia, and in Tertiary times with Malayana, since the Malayan forms with African alliances
are in several cases distinct from those of India. We
know as yet too little of the geology of the eastern
peninsula to say from what epoch dates its connexion
with Indo-Oceanic land. Mr. Theobald has ascertained the existence of Triassic, Cretaceous, and
Nummulitic rocks in the Arabian coast range; and
Carboniferous limestone is known to occur from
Moulmein southward, while the range east of the Ir-
rawadi is formed of younger Tertiary rocks. From
this it would appear that a considerable part of the
Malay peninsula must have been occupied by the sea
during the greater part of the Mesozoic and Eocene
periods. Plant-bearing rocks of Rániganj age have
been identified as forming the outer spurs of the Sik-
kim Himálaya; the ancient land must therefore have
extended some distance to the north of the present
Gangetic delta. Coal both of Cretaceous and Tertiary age occurs in the Khasi hills, and also in Upper
Assam, but in both cases associated with marine
beds; so that it would appear that in this region the
boundaries of land and sea oscillated somewhat during Cretaceous and Eocene times. To the north-west
of India the existence of great formations of Cretaceous and Nummulitic age, stretching far through
Baluchistán and Persia, and entering into the structure of the north-west Himálaya, prove that in the
later Mesozoic and Eocene ages India had no direct
communication with western Asia; while the Jurassic
rocks of Cutch, the Salt range, and the northern
Himálaya, show that in the preceding period the sea

covered a large part of the present Indus basin; and the Triassic, Carboniferous, and still more recent marine formations of the Himálaya, indicate that from very early times till the upheaval of that great chain, much of its present site was for ages covered by the sea.

"To sum up the views advanced in this paper.

"1st. The plant-bearing series of India ranges from early Permian to the latest Jurassic times, indicating (except in a few cases and locally) the uninterrupted continuity of land and fresh water conditions. These may have prevailed from much earlier times.

"2nd. In the early Permian, as in the Postpliocene age, a cold climate prevailed down to low latitudes, and I am inclined to believe in both hemispheres simultaneously. With the decrease of cold the flora and reptilian fauna of Permian times were diffused to Africa, India, and possibly Australia; or the flora may have existed in Australia somewhat earlier, and have been diffused thence.

"3rd. India, South Africa and Australia were connected by an Indo-Oceanic Continent in the Permian epoch; and the two former countries remained connected (with at the utmost only short interruptions) up to the end of the Miocene period. During the latter part of the time this land was also connected with Malayana.

"4th. In common with some previous writers, I consider that the position of this land was defined by the range of coral reefs and banks that now exist between the Arabian sea and East Africa.

"5th. Up to the end of the Nummulitic epoch no

direct connexion (except possibly for short periods) existed between India and Western Asia.''

In the discussion which followed the reading of the paper, Professor Ramsay ''agreed with the author in the belief in the junction of Africa with India and Australia in geological times.''

Mr. Woodward ''was pleased to find that the author had added further evidence, derived from the fossil flora of the mesozoic series of India, in corroboration of the views of Huxley, Sclater and others as to the former existence of an old submerged continent ('Lemuria') which Darwin's researches on coral reefs had long since foreshadowed.''

''Of the five now existing continents,'' writes Ernst Haeckel, in his great work ''The History of Creation,''* ''neither Australia, nor America, nor Europe can have been this primaeval home [of man], or the so-called 'Paradise,' the 'cradle of the human race.' Most circumstances indicate Southern Asia as the locality in question. Besides Southern Asia, the only other of the now existing continents which might be viewed in this light is Africa. But there are a number of circumstances (especially chorological facts) which suggest that the primeval home of man was a continent now sunk below the surface of the Indian Ocean, which extended along the south of Asia, as it is at present (and probably in direct connection with it), towards the east, as far as Further India and the Sunda Islands; towards the west, as far as Madagascar and the south-eastern shores of Af-

*Vol. II., pp. 325-6.

rica. We have already mentioned that many facts in animal and vegetable geography render the former existence of such a South Indian continent very probable. Sclater has given this continent the name of Lemuria, from the semi-apes which were characteristic of it. By assuming this Lemuria to have been man's primaeval home, we greatly facilitate the explanation of the geographical distribution of the human species by migration.''

In a subsequent work, ''The Pedigree of Man,'' Haeckel asserts the existence of Lemuria at some early epoch of the earth's history as an acknowledged fact.

The following quotation from Dr. Hartlaub's writings may bring to a close this portion of the evidence in favour of the existence of the lost Lemuria*:—

''Five and thirty years ago, Isidore Geoffroy St. Hilaire remarked that, if one had to classify the Island of Madagascar exclusively on zoological considerations, and without reference to its geographical situation, it could be shown to be neither Asiatic nor African, but quite different from either, and almost a fourth continent. And this fourth continent could be further proved to be, as regards its fauna, much more different from Africa, which lies so near to it, than from India which is so far away. With these words the correctness and pregnancy of which later investigations tend to bring into their full light, the French naturalist first stated the interesting problem

---

*Dr. G. Hartlaub ''On the Avifauna of Madagascar and the Mascarene Islands,'' see ''The Ibis,'' a Quarterly Journal of Ornithology. Fourth Series, Vol. I., 1877, p. 334.

for the solution of which an hypothesis based on scientific knowledge has recently been propounded, for this fourth continent of Isidore Geoffroy is Sclater's 'Lemuria'—that sunken land which, containing parts of Africa, must have extended far eastwards over Southern India and Ceylon, and the highest points of which we recognise in the volcanic peaks of Bourbon and Mauritius, and in the central range of Madagascar itself—the last resorts of the almost extinct Lemurine race which formerly peopled it.''

Evidence obtained from Archaic Records

The further evidence we have with regard to Lemuria and its inhabitants has been obtained from the same source and in the same manner as that which resulted in the writing of the *Story of Atlantis*. In this case also the author has been privileged to obtain copies of two maps, one representing Lemuria (and the adjoining lands) during the period of that continent's greatest expansion, the other exhibiting its outlines after its dismemberment by great catastrophes, but long before its final destruction.

It was never professed that the maps of Atlantis were correct *to a single degree* of latitude, or longitude, but, with the far greater difficulty of obtaining the information in the present case, it must be stated that still less must these maps of Lemuria be taken as absolutely accurate. In the former case there was a globe, a good bas-relief in terra-cotta, and a well-preserved map on parchment, or skin of some sort, to copy from. In the present case there was only a broken terra-cotta model and a very badly preserved and crumpled map, so that the difficulty of carrying back the remembrance of all the details, and consequently of reproducing exact copies, has been far greater.

We were told that it was by mighty Adepts in the days of Atlantis that the Atlantean maps were produced, but we are not aware whether the Lemurian maps were fashioned by some of the divine instructors in the days when Lemuria still existed, or in still later days of the Atlantean epoch.

But while guarding against over-confidence in the absolute accuracy of the maps in question, the transcriber of the archaic originals believes that they may in all important particulars, be taken as approximately correct.

Probable Duration of the Continent of Lemuria

A period—speaking roughly—of between four and five million years probably represents the life of the continent of Atlantis, for it is about that time since the Rmoahals, the first sub-race of the Fourth Root Race who inhabited Atlantis, arose on a portion of the Lemurian Continent which at that time still existed. Remembering that in the evolutionary process the figure four invariably represents not only the nadir of the cycle, but the period of shortest duration, whether in the case of a Manvantara or of a race, it may be assumed that the number of millions of years assignable as the life-limit of the continent of

Lemuria must be very much greater than that representing the life of Atlantis, the continent of the Fourth Root Race. But in the case of Lemuria no dates can be stated with even approximate accuracy. Geological epochs, so far as they are known to modern science, will be a better medium for contemporary reference, and they alone will be dealt with.

The Maps

But not even geological epochs, it will be observed, are assigned to the maps. If, however, an inference may be drawn from all the evidence before us, it would seem probable that the older of the two Lemurian maps represented the earth's configuration from the Permian, through the Triassic and into the Jurassic epoch, while the second map probably represents the earth's configuration through the Cretaceous and into the Eocene period.

From the older of the two maps it may be seen that the equatorial continent of Lemuria at the time of its greatest expansion nearly girdled the globe, extending as it then did from the site of the present Cape Verd Islands a few miles from the coast of Sierra Leone, in a south-easterly direction through Africa, Australia, the Society Islands and all the intervening seas, to a point but a few miles distant from a great island continent (about the size of the present South America) which spread over the remainder of the Pacific Ocean, and included Cape Horn and parts of Patagonia.

A remarkable feature in the second map of Lemuria is the great length, and at parts the extreme narrowness, of the straits which separated the two great blocks of land into which the continent had by this time been split, and it will be observed that the straits at present existing between the islands of Bali and Lomboc coincide with a portion of the straits which then divided these two continents. It will also be seen that these straits continued in a northerly direction by the west, not by the east coast of Borneo, as conjectured by Ernst Haeckel.

With reference to the distribution of fauna and flora, and the existence of so many types common to India and Africa alike, pointed out by Mr. Blandford, it will be observed that between parts of India and great tracts of Africa there was direct land communication during the first map period, and that similar communication was partially maintained in the second map period also; while a comparison of the maps of Atlantis with those of Lemuria will demonstrate that continuous land communication existed, now at one epoch, and now at another, between so many different parts of the earth's surface, at present separated by sea, that the existing distribution of fauna and flora in the two Americas, in Europe and in Eastern lands, which has been such a puzzle to naturalists, may with perfect ease be accounted for.

The island indicated in the earlier Lemurian map as existing to the north-west of the extreme promontory of that continent, and due west of the present coast of Spain, was probably a centre from which proceeded, during long ages, the distribution of fauna and flora above referred to. For—and this is a most interesting fact—it will be seen that this island must have been the nucleus, from first to last, of the subsequent great continent of Atlantis. It existed, as we see, in these earliest Lemurian times. It was joined in the second map period to land which had previously formed part of the great Lemurian continent; and indeed, so many accretions of territory had it by this time received that it might more appropriately be called a continent than an island. It was the great mountainous region of Atlantis at its prime, when Atlantis embraced great tracts of land which have now become North and South America. It remained the mountainous region of Atlantis in its decadence, and of Ruta in the Ruta and Daitya epoch, and it practically constituted the island of Poseidonis —the last remnant of the continent of Atlantis—the final submergence of which took place in the year 9564 B.C.

A comparison of the two maps here given, along with the four maps of Atlantis, will also show that Australia and New Zealand, Madagascar, parts of Somaliland, the south of Africa, and the extreme southern portion of Patagonia are lands which have *probably* existed through all the intervening catastrophes since the early days of the Lemurian period. The same may be said of the southern parts of India and Ceylon, with the exception in the case of Ceylon, of a temporary submergence in the Ruta and Daitya epoch.

It is true there are also remains still existing of the even earlier Hyperborean continent, and they of course are the oldest known lands on the face of the earth. These are Greenland, Iceland, Spitzbergen, the most northerly parts of Norway and Sweden, and the extreme north cape of Siberia.

Japan is shown by the maps to have been above water, whether as an island, or as part of a continent, since the date of the second Lemurian map. Spain, too, has doubtless existed since that time. Spain is, therefore, with the exception of the most northerly parts of Norway and Sweden, *probably* the oldest land in Europe.

The indeterminate character of the statements just made is rendered necessary by our knowledge that there *did* occur subsidences and upheavals of different portions of the earth's surface during the ages which lay between the periods represented by the maps.

For example, soon after the date of the second Lemurian map we are informed that the whole Malay Peninsula was submerged and remained so for a long time, but a subsequent upheaval of that region must have taken place before the date of the first Atlantean map, for, what is now the Malay Peninsula is there exhibited as part of a great continent. Similarly there have been repeated minor subsidences and upheavals nearer home in more recent times, and Haeckel is perfectly correct in saying that England—he might with greater accuracy have said the islands of Great Britain and Ireland, which were then joined together—"has repeatedly been connected with the European continent, and been repeatedly separated from it."

In order to bring the subject more clearly before the mind, a tabular statement is here annexed which supplies a condensed history of the animal and plant life on our globe, bracketed—according to Haeckel —with the contemporary rock strata. Two other columns give the contemporary races of man, and such of the great cataclysms as are known to occult students.

Reptiles and Pine Forests

From this statement it will be seen that Lemurian man lived in the age of Reptiles and Pine Forests. The amphibious monsters and the gigantic tree-ferns of the Permian age still flourished in the warm damp climates. Plesiosauri and Icthyosauri swarmed in the tepid marshes of the Mesolithic epoch, but, with the drying up of many of the inland seas, the Dinosauria —the monstrous land reptiles—gradually became the dominant type, while the Pterodactyls—the Saurians which developed bat-like wings—not only crawled on the earth, but flew through the air. The smallest of these latter were about the size of a sparrow; the largest, however, with a breadth of wing of more than sixteen feet, exceeding the largest of our living birds of to-day; while most of the Dinosauria —the Dragons—were terrible beasts of prey, colossal reptiles which attained a length of from forty to fifty feet.* Subsequent excavations have laid bare skeletons of an even larger size. Professor Ray Lankester at a meeting of the Royal Institution on 7th January,

*Ernst Haeckel's "History of Creation," Vol. II., pp. 22-56.

1904, is reported to have referred to a brontosaurus skeleton of sixty-five feet long, which had been discovered in the Oolite deposit in the southern part of the United States of America.

As it is written in the stanzas of the archaic Book of Dzyan, "Animals with bones, dragons of the deep, and flying sarpas were added to the creeping things. They that creep on the ground got wings. They of the long necks in the water became the progenitors of the fowls of the air." Modern science records her endorsement. "The class of birds as already remarked is so closely allied to Reptiles in internal structure and by embryonal development that they undoubtedly originated out of a branch of this class. . . . The derivation of birds from reptiles first took place in the Mesolithic epoch, and this moreover probably during the Trias."*

In the vegetable kingdom this epoch also saw the pine and the palm-tree gradually displace the giant tree ferns. In the later days of the Mesolithic epoch, mammals for the first time came into existence, but the fossil remains of the mammoth and mastodon, which were their earliest representatives, are chiefly found in the subsequent strata of the Eocene and Miocene times.

The Human Kingdom

Before making any reference to what must, even at this early date, be called the human kingdom, it

---

*Ernst Haeckel's "History of Creation," Vol. II., pp. 226-7.

must be stated that none of those who, at the present day, can lay claim to even a moderate amount of mental or spiritual culture *can* have lived in these ages. It was only with the advent of the last three sub-races of this Third Root Race that the least progressed of the first group of the Lunar Pitris began to return to incarnation, while the most advanced among them did not take birth till the early sub-races of the Atlantean period.

Indeed, Lemurian man, during at least the first half of the race, must be regarded rather as an animal destined to reach humanity than as human according to our understanding of the term; for though the second and third groups of Pitris, who constituted the inhabitants of Lemuria during its first four sub-races, had achieved sufficient self-consciousness in the Lunar Manvantara to differentiate them from the animal kingdom, they had not yet received the Divine Spark which should endow them with mind and individuality—in other words, make them truly human.

Size and Consistency of Man's Body

The evolution of this Lemurian race, therefore, constitutes one of the most obscure, as well as one of the most interesting, chapters of man's development, for during this period not only did he reach true humanity, but his body underwent the greatest physical changes, while the processes of reproduction were twice altered.

In explanation of the surprising statements which

Rock Strata		Depth of Strata Feet	Races of Men	Cataclysms	Animals	Plants
Laurentian Cambrian Silurian	Archilithic or Primordial	70,000	First Root Race which being Astral could leave no fossil remains		Skull-less Animals	Forests of gigantic Tangles and other Thallus Plants
Devonian Coal Permian	Palaeolithic or Primary	42,000	Second Root Race which was Etheric		Fish	Fern Forests
Triassic Jurassic Cretaceous	Mesolithic or Secondary	15,000	Third Root Race or Lemurian	Lemuria is said to have perished before the beginning of the Eocene age.	Reptiles	Pine and Palm Forests
Eocene Miocene Pliocene	Cenolithic or Tertiary	5,000	Fourth Root Race or Atlantean	The main Continent of Atlantis was destroyed in the Miocene period about 800,000 years ago. Second great catastrophe ? about 200,000 years ago.	Mammals	Forests of Deciduous Trees
Diluvial or Pleistocene Alluvial	Quarternary or Anthopolithic	500	Fifth Root Race or Aryan	Third great catastrophe about 80,000 years ago. Final submergence of Poseidonis 9564 B.C.	More differentiated Mammals	Cultivated Forests

will have to be made in regard to the size and consistency of man's body at this early period it must be remembered that while the animal, vegetable and mineral kingdoms pursued the normal course, on this the fourth globe, during the Fourth Round of this Manvantara, it was ordained that humanity should run over in rapid succession the various stages through which its evolution had passed during the previous rounds of the present Manvantara. Thus the bodies of the First Root Race in which these almost mindless beings were destined to gain experience, would have appeared to us as gigantic phantoms—if indeed we could have seen them at all, for their bodies were formed of astral matter. The astral forms of the First Root Race were then gradually enveloped in a more physical casing. But though the Second Root Race may be called physical—their bodies being composed of ether—they would have been equally invisible to eyesight as it at present exists.

It was, we are told, in order that the Manu, and the Beings who aided him, might take means for improving the physical type of humanity that this epitome of the process of evolution was ordained. The highest development which the type had so far reached was the huge ape-like creature which had existed on the three physical planets, Mars, the Earth and Mercury in the Third Round. On the arrival of the human life-wave on the Earth in this the Fourth Round, a certain number, naturally, of these ape-like creatures were found in occupation—the residuum left on the planet during its period of obscuration. These, of course, joined the in-coming human stream as soon as the race became fully physical. Their bodies may not then have been absolutely discarded; they may have been utilized for purposes of reincarnation for the most backward entities, but it was an improvement on this type which was required, and this was most easily achieved by the Manu, through working out on the astral plane in the first instance, the architype originally formed in the mind of the Logos.

From the Etheric Second Race, then, was evolved the Third—the Lemurian. Their bodies had become material, being composed of the gases, liquids and solids which constitute the three lowest sub-divisions of the physical plane, but the gases and liquids still predominated, for as yet their vertebrate structure had not solidified into bones such as ours, and they could not, therefore, stand erect. Their bones in fact were pliable as the bones of young infants now are. It was not until the middle of the Lemurian period that man developed a solid bony structure.

To explain the possibility of the process by which the etheric form evolved into a more physical form, and the soft-boned physical form ultimately developed into a structure such as man possesses to-day, it is only necessary to refer to the permanent physical atom.* Containing as it does the essence of all the forms through which man has passed on the physical plane, it contained consequently the potentiality of a hard-boned physical structure such as had been at-

---

*For a further account of the permanent atoms on all the planes, and the potentialities contained in them with reference to the processes of death and re-birth, see ''Man's Place in Universe,'' pp. 76-80.

tained during the course of the Third Round, as well as the potentiality of an etheric form and all the phases which lie between, for it must be remembered that the physical plane consists of four grades of ether as well as the gases, liquids and solids which so many are apt to regard as alone constituting the physical. Thus, every stage of the development was a natural process, for it was a process which had been accomplished in ages long past, and all that was needed was for the Manu and the Beings who aided him, to gather round the permanent atom the appropriate kind of matter.

Organs of Vision

The organs of vision of these creatures before they developed bones were of a rudimentary nature, at least such was the condition of the two eyes in front with which they sought for their food upon the ground. But there was a third eye at the back of the head, the atrophied remnant of which is now known as the *pineal gland.* This, as we know, is *now* a centre solely of astral vision, but at the epoch of which we are speaking it was the chief centre not only of astral but of physical sight. Referring to reptiles which had become extinct, Professor Ray Lankester, in a recent lecture at the Royal Institution, is reported to have drawn special attention ''to the size of the parietal foramen in the skull which showed that in the ichthyosaurs the parietal or pineal eye on the top of the head must have been very large.'' In this respect he went on to say mankind were inferior to these big sea lizards, ''for we had lost the third eye which might be studied in the common lizard, or better in the great blue lizard of the South of France.''*

Somewhat before the middle of the Lemurian period, probably during the evolution of the third sub-race, the gigantic gelatinous body began slowly to solidify and the soft-boned limbs developed into a bony structure. These primitive creatures were now able to stand upright, and the two eyes in the face gradually became the chief organs of physical sight, though the third eye still remained to some extent an organ of physical sight also, and this it did till the very end of the Lemurian epoch. It, of course, remained an actual organ, as it still is a potential focus, of psychic vision. This psychic vision continued to be an attribute of the race not only throughout the whole Lemurian period, but well into the days of Atlantis.

A curious fact to note is that when the race first attained the power of standing and moving in an upright position, they could walk backwards with almost as great ease as forwards. This may be accounted for not only by the capacity for vision possessed by the third eye, but doubtless also by the curious projection at the heels which will presently be referred to.

Description of Lemurian Man

The following is a description of a man who belonged to one of the later sub-races—probably the fifth.

*The ''Standard,'' 8th Jan., 1904.

"His stature was gigantic, somewhere between twelve and fifteen feet. His skin was very dark, being of a yellowish brown colour. He had a long lower jaw, a strangely flattened face, eyes small but piercing and set curiously far apart, so that he could see sideways as well as in front, while the eye at the back of the head—on which part of the head no hair, of course, grew—enabled him to see in that direction also. He had no forehead, but there seemed to be a roll of flesh where it should have been. The head sloped backwards and upwards in a rather curious way. The arms and legs (especially the former) were longer in proportion than ours, and could not be perfectly straightened either at elbows or knees; the hands and feet were enormous, and the heels projected backwards in an ungainly way. The figure was draped in a loose robe of skin, something like rhinoceros hide, but more scaly, probably the skin of some animal of which we now know only through its fossil remains. Round his head, on which the hair was quite short, was twisted another piece of skin to which were attached tassels of bright red, blue and other colours. In his left hand he held a sharpened staff, which was doubtless used for defence or attack. It was about the height of his own body, *viz.*, twelve to fifteen feet. In his right hand was twisted the end of a long rope made of some sort of creeping plant, by which he led a huge and hideous reptile, somewhat resembling the Plesiosaurus. The Lemurians actually domesticated these creatures, and trained them to employ their strength in hunting other animals. The appearance of the man gave an unpleasant sensation, but he was not entirely uncivilised, being an average common-place specimen of his day."

Many were even less human in appearance than the individual here described, but the seventh sub-race developed a superior type, though very unlike any living men of the present time. While retaining the projecting lower jaw, the thick heavy lips, the flattened face, and the uncanny looking eyes, they had by this time developed something which might be called a forehead, while the curious projection of the heel had been considerably reduced. In one branch of this seventh sub-race, the head might be described as almost egg-shaped—the small end of the egg being uppermost, with the eyes wide apart and very near the top. The stature had perceptibly decreased, and the appearance of the hands, feet and limbs generally had become more like those of the negroes of to-day. These people developed an important and long-lasting civilisation, and for thousands of years dominated most of the other tribes who dwelt on the vast Lemurian continent, and even at the end, when racial decay seemed to be overtaking them, they secured another long lease of life and power by inter-marriage with the Rmoahals—the first sub-race of the Atlanteans. The progeny, while retaining many Third Race characteristics, of course, really belonged to the Fourth Race, and thus naturally acquired fresh power of development. Their general appearance now became not unlike that of some American Indians, except that their skin had a curious bluish tinge not now to be seen.

But surprising as were the changes in the size, consistency, and appearance of man's body during this period, the alterations in the process of reproduction are still more astounding. A reference to the systems which now obtain among the lower kingdoms of nature may help us in the consideration of the subject.

Processes of Reproduction

After instancing the simplest processes of propagation by self-division, and by the formation of buds (Gemmatio), Haeckel proceeds, "A third mode of non-sexual propagation, that of the formation of germ-buds (Polysporogonia) is intimately connected with the formation of buds. In the case of the lower, imperfect organisms, among animals, especially in the case of the plant-like animals and worms, we very frequently find that in the interior of an individual composed of many cells, a small group of cells separates itself from those surrounding it, and that this small isolated group gradually develops itself into an individual, which becomes like the parent and sooner or later comes out of it. . . . The formation of germ buds is evidently but little different from real budding. But, on the other hand, it is connected with a fourth kind of non-sexual propagation, which almost forms a transition to sexual reproduction, namely, the formation of germ cells (Monosporogonia). In this case it is no longer a group of cells but a single cell, which separates itself from the surrounding cells in the interior of the producing organism, and which becomes further developed after it has come out of its parent. . . . Sexual or amphigonic propagation (Amphigonia) is the usual method of propagation among all higher animals and plants. It is evident that it has only developed at a very late

period of the earth's history, from non-sexual propagation, and apparently in the first instance from the
method of propagation by germ-cells. . . . In all the
chief forms of non-sexual propagation mentioned
above—in fission, in the formation of buds, germ-
buds, and germ-cells—the separated cell or group of
cells was able by itself to develop into a new individual, but in the case of sexual propagation, the cell
must first be fructified by another generative substance. The fructifying sperm must first mix with the
germ-cell (the egg) before the latter can develop into
a new individual. These two generative substances,
the sperm and the egg, are either produced by one
and the same individual hermaphrodite (Hermaph-
roditismus) or by two different individuals (sexual-
separation).

"The simpler and more ancient form of sexual
propagation is through double-sexed individuals.
It occurs in the great majority of plants, but only
in a minority of animals, for example, in the garden snails, leeches, earth-worms, and many other
worms. Every single individual among hermaphrodites produces within itself materials of both sexes—
eggs and sperm. In most of the higher plants every
blossom contains both the male organ (stamens and
anther) and the female organ (style and germ). Every
garden snail produces in one part of its sexual gland
eggs, and in another part sperm. Many hermaphrodites can fructify themselves; in others, however,
reciprocal fructification of both hermaphrodites is
necessary for causing the development of the eggs.
This latter case is evidently a transition to sexual
separation.

"Sexual separation, which characterises the more

complicated of the two kinds of sexual reproduction, has evidently been developed from the condition of hermaphroditism at a late period of the organic history of the world. It is at present the universal method of propagation of the higher animals. . . . The so-called virginal reproduction (Parthenogenesis) offers an interesting form of transition from sexual reproduction to the nonsexual formation of germ-cells which most resembles it. . . . In this case germ-cells which otherwise appear and are formed exactly like egg-cells, become capable of developing themselves into new individuals without requiring the fructifying seed. The most remarkable and the most instructive of the different parthenogenetic phenomena are furnished by those cases in which the same germ-cells, according as they are fructified or not, produce different kinds of individuals. Among our common honey bees, a male individual (a drone) arises out of the eggs of the queen, if the egg has not been fructified; a female (a queen, or working bee) if the egg has been fructified. It is evident from this, that in reality there exists no wide chasm between sexual and non-sexual reproduction, but that both modes of reproduction are directly connected."*

Now, the interesting fact in connection with the evolution of Third Race man on Lemuria, is that his mode of reproduction ran through phases which were closely analogous with some of the processes above described. Sweat-born, egg-born and Androgyne are the terms used in the Secret Doctrine.

"Almost sexless, in its early beginnings, it became bisexual or androgynous; very gradually, of course.

*Ernst Haeckel's "The History of Creation," 2nd ed., Vol. I., pp. 193-8.

The passage from the former to the latter transformation required numberless generations, during which the simple cell that issued from the earliest parent (the two in one), first developed into a bisexual being; and then the cell, becoming a regular egg, gave forth a unisexual creature. The Third Race mankind is the most mysterious of all the hitherto developed five Races. The mystery of the "How" of the generation of the distinct sexes must, of course, be very obscure here, as it is the business of an embryologist and a specialist, the present work giving only faint outlines of the process. But it is evident that the units of the Third Race humanity began to separate in their pre-natal shells, or eggs, and to issue out of them as distinct male and female babes, ages after the appearance of its early progenitors. And, as time rolled on its geological periods, the newly born sub-races began to lose their natal capacities. Toward the end of the fourth *sub-race,* the babe lost its faculty of walking as soon as liberated from its shell, and by the end of the fifth, mankind was born under the same conditions and by the same identical process as our historical generations. This required, of course, millions of years.''*

Lemurian Races Still Inhabiting the Earth

It may be as well again to repeat that the almost mindless creatures who inhabited such bodies as

*"The Secret Doctrine," Vol. II., p. 197. (In the original 2-volume edition, Adyar: Theosophical Publishing House, 1888 —ED.)

have been above described during the early sub-races of the Lemurian period can scarcely be regarded as completely human. It was only after the separation of the sexes, when their bodies had become densely physical, that they became human even in appearance. It must be remembered that the beings we are speaking of, though embracing the second and third groups of the Lunar Pitris, must also have been largely recruited from the animal kingdom of that (the Lunar) Manvantara. The degraded remnants of the Third Root Race who still inhabit the earth may be recognised in the aborigines of Australia, the Andaman Islanders, some hill tribes of India, the Tierra-del-Fuegans, the Bushmen of Africa, and some other savage tribes.* The entities now inhabiting these bodies must have belonged to the animal kingdom in the early part of *this* Manvantara. It was probably during the evolution of the Lemurian race and before the "door was shut" on the entities thronging up from below, that these attained the human kingdom.

Sin of the Mindless

The shameful acts of the mindless men at the first separation of the sexes had best be referred to in the words of the stanzas of the archaic Book of Dzyan. No commentary is needed.

"During the Third Race the boneless animals

---

*"Savage" was used at the time of this writing to mean "primitive."—ED.

grew and changed, they became animals with bones, their chayas became solid.

"The animals separated first. They began to breed. The two-fold man separated also. He said, 'Let us as they; let us unite and make creatures.' They did.

"And those that had no spark took huge she-animals unto them. They begat upon them dumb races. Dumb they were themselves. But their tongues untied. The tongues of their progeny remained still. Monsters they bred. A race of crooked red-hair-covered monsters going on all fours. A dumb race to keep the shame untold. (And an ancient commentary adds 'when the Third separated and fell into sin by breeding men-animals, these (the animals) became ferocious, and men and they mutually destructive. Till then, there was no sin, no life taken.')

"Seeing which the Lhas who had not built men, wept, saying. 'The Amanasa [mindless] have defiled our future abodes. This is Karma. Let us dwell in the others. Let us teach them better lest worse should happen.' They did.

"Then all men became endowed with Manas. They saw the sin of the mindless."

Origin of the Pithecoid and the Anthropoid Apes

The anatomical resemblance between Man and the higher Ape, so frequently cited by Darwinists as pointing to some ancestor common to both, presents an interesting problem, the proper solution of which is to be sought for in the esoteric explanation of the genesis of the pithecoid stocks.

Now, we gather from the Secret Doctrine* that the descendants of these semi-human monsters described above as originating in the sin of the "mindless," having through long centuries dwindled in size and become more densely physical, culminated in a race of Apes at the time of the Miocene period, from which in their turn are descended the pithecoids of to-day. With these Apes of the Miocene period, however, the Atlanteans of that age renewed the sin of the "mindless"—this time with full responsibility, and the resultants of their crime are the species of Apes now known as Anthropoid.

We are given to understand that in the coming Sixth Root Race, these anthropoids will obtain human incarnation, in the bodies doubtless of the lowest races then existing upon earth.

That part of the Lemurian continent where the separation of the sexes took place, and where both the fourth and the fifth sub-races flourished, is to be found in the earlier of the two maps. It lay to the east of the mountainous region of which the present Island of Madagascar formed a part, and thus occupied a central position around the smaller of the two great lakes.

Origin of Language

As stated in the stanzas of Dzyan above quoted, the men of that epoch, even though they had become completely physical, still remained speechless. Naturally the astral and etherial ancestors of this Third

*Vol. II., pp. 683 and 689.

Root Race had no need to produce a series of sounds in order to convey their thoughts, living as they did in astral and etherial conditions, but when man became physical he could not for long remain dumb. We are told that the sounds which these primitive men made to express their thoughts were at first composed entirely of vowels. In the slow course of evolution the consonant sounds gradually came into use, but the development of language from first to last on the continent of Lemuria never reached beyond the monosyllabic phase. The Chinese language of to-day is the sole great lineal descendant of ancient Lemurian speech* for "the whole human race was at that time of one language and of one lip."†

In Humboldt's classification of language, the Chinese, as we know, is called the *isolating* as distinguished from the more highly evolved *agglutinative,* and the still more highly evolved *inflectional.* Readers of the *Story of Atlantis* may remember that many different languages were developed on that continent, but all belonged to the *agglutinative,* or, as Max Müller prefers to call it, the *combinatory* type, while the still higher development of *inflectional* speech, in the Aryan and Semitic tongues, was reserved for our own era of the Fifth Root Race.

The First Taking of Life

The first instance of sin, the first taking of life— quoted above from an old commentary on the stanzas

---

*It must, however, be noted that the Chinese *people* are mainly descended from the fourth or Turanian sub-race of the Fourth Root Race.

†"Secret Doctrine," Vol. II., p. 198.

of Dzyan, may be taken as indicative of the attitude which was then inaugurated between the human and the animal kingdom, and which has since attained such awful proportions, not only between men and animals, but between the different races of men themselves. And this opens up a most interesting avenue of thought.

The fact that Kings and Emperors consider it necessary or appropriate, on all state occasions, to appear in the garb of one of the fighting branches of their service, is a significant indication of the apotheosis reached by the combative qualities in man! The custom doubtless comes down from a time when the King was the warrior-chief, and when his kingship was acknowledged solely in virtue of his being the chief warrior. But now that the Fifth Root Race is in ascendency, whose chief characteristic and function is the development of intellect, it might have been expected that the dominant attribute of the Fourth Root Race would have been a little less conspicuously paraded. But the era of one race overlaps another, and though, as we know, the leading races of the world all belong to the Fifth Root Race, the vast majority of its inhabitants still belong to the Fourth, and it would appear that the Fifth Root Race has not yet outstripped Fourth Race characteristics, for it is by infinitely slow degrees that man's evolution is accomplished.

It will be interesting here to summarise the history of this strife and bloodshed from its genesis during these far-off ages on Lemuria.

From the information placed before the writer it would seem that the antagonism between men and animals was developed first. With the evolution of

man's physical body, suitable food for that body naturally became an urgent need, so that in addition to
the antagonism brought about by the necessity of
self-defence against the now ferocious animals, the
desire of food also urged men to their slaughter, and
as we have seen above, one of the first uses they
made of their budding mentality was to train animals
to act as hunters in the chase.

The element of strife having once been kindled,
men soon began to use weapons of offence against
each other. The causes of aggression were naturally
the same as those which exist to-day among savage
communities. The possession of any desirable object
by one of his fellows was sufficient inducement for a
man to attempt to take it by force. Nor was strife
limited to single acts of aggression. As among
savages to-day, bands of marauders would attack
and pillage the communities who dwelt at a distance
from their own village. But to this extent only, we
are told, was warfare organised on Lemuria, even
down to the end of its seventh sub-race.

It was reserved for the Atlanteans to develop the
principle of strife on organised lines—to collect and
to drill armies and to build navies. This principle of
strife was indeed the fundamental characteristic of
the Fourth Root Race. All through the Atlantean
period, as we know, warfare was the order of the
day, and battles were constantly fought on land and
sea. And so deeply rooted in man's nature during the
Atlantean period did this principle of strife become,
that even now the most intellectually developed of
the Aryan races are ready to war upon each other.

The Arts

To trace the development of the Arts among the Lemurians, we must start with the history of the fifth
sub-race. The separation of the sexes was now fully
accomplished, and man inhabited a completely physical body, though it was still of gigantic stature. The
offensive and defensive war with the monstrous
beasts of prey had already begun, and men had
taken to living in huts. To build their huts they tore
down trees, and piled them up in a rude fashion. At
first each separate family lived in its own clearing in
the jungle, but they soon found it safer, as a defence
against the wild beasts, to draw together and live in
small communities. Their huts, too, which had been
formed of rude trunks of trees, they now learnt to
build with boulders of stone, while the weapons with
which they attacked, or defended themselves against
the Dinosauria and other wild beasts, were spears of
sharpened wood, similar to the staff held by the man
whose appearance is described above.

Up to this time agriculture was unknown, and the
uses of fire had not been discovered. The food of
their boneless ancestors who crawled on the earth
were such things as they could find on the surface of
the ground or just below it. Now that they walked
erect many of the wild forest trees provided them
with nuts and berries, but their chief article of food
was the flesh of the beasts and reptiles which they
slew, tore in pieces, and devoured.

Teachers of the Lemurian Race

But now there occurred an event pregnant with consequences the most momentous in the history of the human race. An event too full of mystical import, for its narration brings into view Beings who belonged to entirely different systems of evolution, and who nevertheless came at this epoch to be associated with our humanity.

The lament of the Lhas "who had not built men" at seeing their future abodes defiled, is at first sight far from intelligible. Though the descent of these Beings into human bodies is not the chief event to which we have to refer, some explanation of its cause and its result must first be attempted. Now, we are given to understand that these Lhas were the highly evolved humanity of some system of evolution which had run its course at a period in the infinitely far-off past. They had reached a high stage of development on their chain of worlds, and since its dissolution had passed the intervening ages in the bliss of some Nirvanic condition. But their karma now necessitated a return to some field of action and of physical causes, and as they had not yet fully learnt the lesson of compassion, their temporary task now lay in becoming guides and teachers of the Lemurian race, who then required all the help and guidance they could get.

But other Beings also took up the task—in this case voluntarily. These came from the scheme of evolution which has Venus as its one physical planet. That scheme has already reached the Seventh Round of its planets in its Fifth Manvantara; its humanity therefore stands at a far higher level than ordinary mankind on this earth has yet attained. They are "divine" while we are only "human." The Lemurians, as we have seen, were then merely on the verge of attaining true manhood. It was to supply a temporary need—the education of our infant humanity—that these divine Beings came—as we possibly, long ages hence, may similarly be called to give a helping hand to the beings struggling up to manhood on the Jupiter or the Saturn chain. Under their guidance and influence the Lemurians rapidly advanced in mental growth. The stirring of their minds with feelings of love and reverence for those whom they felt to be infinitely wiser and greater than themselves naturally resulted in efforts of imitation, and so the necessary advance in mental growth was achieved which transformed the higher mental sheath into a vehicle capable of carrying over the human characteristics from life to life, thus warranting that outpouring of the Divine Life which endowed the recipient with individual immortality. As expressed in the archaic stanzas of Dzyan, "Then all men became endowed with Manas."

A great distinction, however, must be noted between the coming of the exalted Beings from the Venus scheme and that of those described as the highly evolved humanity of some previous system of evolution. The former, as we have seen, were under no karmic impulse. They came as men to live and work among them, but they were not required to assume their physical limitations, being in a position to provide appropriate vehicles for themselves.

The Lhas on the other hand had actually to be born in the bodies of the race as it then existed. Better would it have been both for them and for the race if there had been no hesitation or delay on their part in taking up their Karmic task, for the sin of the mindless and all its consequences would have been avoided. Their task, too, would have been an easier one, for it consisted not only in acting as guides and teachers, but in improving the racial type—in short, in evolving out of the half-human, half-animal form then existing, the physical body of the man to be.

It must be remembered that up to this time the Lemurian race consisted of the second and third groups of the Lunar Pitris. But now that they were approaching the level reached on the Lunar chain by the first group of Pitris, it became necessary for these again to return to incarnation, and this they did all through the fifth, sixth and seventh sub-races (indeed, some did not take birth till the Atlantean period), so that the impetus given to the progress of the race was a cumulative force.

The positions occupied by the divine beings from the Venus chain were naturally those of rulers, instructors in religion, and teachers of the arts, and it is in this latter capacity that a reference to the arts taught by them comes to our aid in the consideration of the history of this early race.

The Arts continued

Under the guidance of their divine teachers the people began to learn the use of fire, and the means by which it could be obtained, at first by friction, and later on by the use of flints and iron. They were taught to explore for metals, to smelt and to mould them, and instead of spears of sharpened wood they now began to use spears tipped with sharpened metal.

They were also taught to dig and till the ground and to cultivate the seeds of wild grain till it improved in type. This cultivation carried on through the vast ages which have since elapsed has resulted in the evolution of the various cereals which we now possess—barley, oats, maize, millet, etc. But an exception must here be noted. Wheat was not evolved upon this planet like the other cereals. It was a gift of the divine beings who brought it from Venus ready for the food of man. Nor was wheat their only gift. The one animal form whose type has not been evolved on our chain of worlds is that of the bee. It, too, was brought from Venus.

The Lemurians now also began to learn the art of spinning and weaving fabrics with which to clothe themselves. These were made of the coarse hair of a species of animal now extinct, but which bore some resemblance to the llamas of to-day, the ancestors of which they may possibly have been. We have seen above that the earliest articles of clothing of Lemurian man were robes of skin stripped from the beasts he had slain. These skins he still continued to wear on the colder parts of the continent, but he now learnt to cure and dress the skin in some rude fashion.

One of the first things the people were taught was the use of fire in the preparation of their food, and whether it was the flesh of animals they slew or the pounded grains of wheat, their modes of cooking were closely analogous to those we hear of as existing to-day among savage communities. With reference to the gift of wheat so marvellously brought from Venus, the divine rulers doubtless realised the advisability of at once procuring such food for the people, for they must have known that it would take many generations before the cultivation of the wild seeds could provide an adequate supply.

Rude and barbarous as were the people during the period of the fifth and sixth sub-races, such of them as had the privilege of coming in contact with their divine teachers were naturally inspired with such feelings of reverence and worship as helped to lift them out of their savage condition. The constant influx, too, of more intelligent beings from the first group of the Lunar Pitris, who were then beginning to return to incarnation, helped the attainment of a more civilised state.

Great Cities and Statues

During the later part of the sixth, and the seventh sub-race they learnt to build great cities. These appear to have been of cyclopean architecture, corresponding with the gigantic bodies of the race. The first cities were built on that extended mountainous region of the continent which included, as will be seen in the first map, the present Island of Madagascar. Another great city is described in the "Secret

Doctrine''* as having been entirely built of blocks of lava. It lay some 30 miles west of the present Easter Island, and it was subsequently destroyed by a series of volcanic eruptions. The gigantic statues of Easter Island—measuring as most of them do about 27 feet in height by 8 feet across the shoulders—were probably intended to be representative not only of the features, but of the height of those who carved them, or it may be of their ancestors, for it was probably in the later ages of the Lemuro-Atlanteans that the statues were erected. It will be observed that by the second map period, the continent of which Easter Island formed a part had been broken up and Easter Island itself had become a comparatively small island, though of considerably greater dimensions than it retains to-day.

Civilisations of comparative importance arose on different parts of the continent and the great islands where the inhabitants built cities and dwelt in settled communities, but large tribes who were also partially civilised continued to lead a nomadic and patriarchial life; while other parts of the land—in many cases the least accessible, as in our own times—were peopled by tribes of extremely low type.

Religion

With so primitive a race of men, at the best, there was but little in the shape of religion that they could

*Vol. II., p. 317.

be taught. Simple rules of conduct and the most elementary precepts of morality were all that they were fitted to understand or to practise. During the evolution of the seventh sub-race, it is true that their divine instructors taught them some primitive form of worship and imparted the knowledge of a Supreme Being whose symbol was represented as the Sun.

Destruction of the Continent

Unlike the subsequent fate of Atlantis, which was submerged by great tidal waves, the continent of Lemuria perished by volcanic action. It was raked by the burning ashes and the red-hot dust from numberless volcanoes. Earthquakes and volcanic eruptions, it is true, heralded each of the great catastrophes which overtook Atlantis, but when the land had been shaken and rent, the sea rushed in and completed the work, and most of the inhabitants perished by drowning. The Lemurians, on the other hand, met their doom chiefly by fire or suffocation. Another marked contrast between the fate of Lemuria and Atlantis was that while four great catastrophes completed the destruction of the latter, the former was slowly eaten away by internal fires, for, from the time when the disintegrating process began towards the end of the first map period, there was no cessation from the fiery activity, and whether in one part of the continent or another, the volcanic action was incessant, while the invariable sequence was the subsidence and total disappearance of the land, just as in the case of Krakatoa in 1883.

So closely analogous was the eruption of Mount Pelée, which caused the destruction of St. Pièrre, the capital of Martinique, about two years ago, to the whole series of volcanic catastrophes on the continent of Lemuria, that the description of the former given by some of the survivors may be of interest. "An immense black cloud had suddenly burst forth from the crater of Mont Pelée and rushed with terrific velocity upon the city, destroying everything—inhabitants, houses and vegetation alike—that it found in its path. In two or three minutes it passed over, and the city was a blazing pyre of ruins. In both islands [Martinique and St. Vincent] the eruptions were characterised by the sudden discharge of immense quantities of red-hot dust, mixed with steam, which flowed down the steep hillsides with an ever-increasing velocity. In St. Vincent this had filled many valleys to a depth of between 100 feet and 200 feet, and months after the eruptions was still very hot, and the heavy rains which then fell thereon caused enormous explosions, producing clouds of steam and dust that shot upwards to a height of from 1500 feet to 2000 feet, and filled the rivers with black boiling mud." Captain Freeman, of the "Roddam," then described "a thrilling experience which he and his party had at Martinique. One night, when they were lying at anchor in a little sloop about a mile from St. Pièrre, the mountain exploded in a way that was apparently an exact repetition of the original eruption. It was not entirely without warning; hence they were enabled to sail at once a mile or two further away, and thus probably saved their lives. In the darkness they saw the summit glow with a bright red light; then soon, with loud detonations, great red-hot stones were projected into the air and rolled down the slopes. A few minutes later a prolonged rumbling noise was heard, and in an instant was followed by a red-hot avalanche of dust, which rushed out of the crater and rolled down the side with a terrific speed, which they estimated at about 100 miles an hour, with a temperature of 1000° centigrade. As to the probable explanation of these phenomena, no lava, he said, had been seen to flow from either of the volcanoes, but only steam and fine hot dust. The volcanoes were, therefore, of the explosive type; and from all his observations he had concluded that the absence of lava-flows was due to the material within the crater being partly solid, or at least highly viscous, so that it could not flow like an ordinary lava-stream. Since his return this theory had received striking confirmation, for it was now known that within the crater of Mont Pelée there was no lake of molten lava, but that a solid pillar of red-hot rock was slowly rising upwards in a great conical, sharp-pointed hill, until it might finally overtop the old summit of the mountain. It was nearly 1000 feet high, and slowly grew as it was forced upwards by pressure from beneath, while every now and then explosions of steam took place, dislodging large pieces from its summit or its sides. Steam was set free within this mass as it cooled, and the rock then passed into a dangerous and highly explosive condition, such that an explosion must sooner or later take place, which shivered a great part of the mass into fine red-hot dust.''*

A reference to the first Lemurian map will show that in the lake lying to the south-east of the extensive mountainous region there was an island which consisted of little more than one great mountain. This mountain was a very active volcano. The four mountains which lay to the south-west of the lake were also active volcanoes, and in this region it was that the disruption of the continent began. The seismic cataclysms which followed the volcanic eruptions caused such wide-spread damage that by the second map period a large portion of the southern part of the continent had been submerged.

A marked characteristic of the land surface in early Lemurian times was the great number of lakes and marshes, as well as the innumerable volcanoes. Of course, all these are not shown on the map. Only some of the great mountains which were volcanoes, and only some of the largest lakes are there indicated.

Another volcano on the north-east coast of the continent began its destructive work at an early date. Earthquakes completed the disruption, and it seems probable that the sea shown in the second map as dotted with small islands to the south-east of the present Japan, indicates the area of seismic disturbance.

In the first map it will be seen that there were lakes in the centre of what is now the island-continent of Australia—lakes where the land is at present exceed-

*The ''Times,'' 14th Sept., 1903.

ingly dry and parched. By the second map period those lakes had disappeared, and it seems natural to conjecture that the districts where those lakes lay, must, during the eruptions of the great volcanoes which lay to the south-east (between the present Australia and New Zealand), have been so raked with red-hot volcanic dust that the very water-springs were dried up.

Founding of the Atlantean Race

In concluding this sketch, a reference to the process by which the Fourth Root Race was brought into existence, will appropriately bring to an end what we know of the story of Lemuria and link it on to that of Atlantis.

It may be remembered from previous writings on the subject that it was from the *fifth* or Semitic sub-race of the Fourth Root Race that was chosen the nucleus destined to become our great Fifth or Aryan Root Race. It was not, however, until the time of the *seventh* sub-race on Lemuria that humanity was sufficiently developed physiologically to warrant the choice of individuals fit to become the parents of a new Root Race. So it was from the seventh sub-race that the segregation was effected. The colony was first settled on land which occupied the site of the present Ashantee and Western Nigeria. A reference to the second map will show this as a promontory lying to the north-west of the island-continent which embraced the Cape of Good Hope and parts of

western Africa. Having been guarded for generations from any admixture with a lower type, the colony gradually increased in numbers, and the time
came when it was ready to receive and to hand on the
new impulse to physical heredity which the Manu
was destined to impart.

Students of Theosophy are aware that, up to the
present day, no one belonging to our humanity has
been in a position to undertake the exalted office of
Manu, though it is stated that the founding of the
coming Sixth Root Race will be entrusted to the guidance of one of our Masters of Wisdom—one who,
while belonging to our humanity, has nevertheless
reached a most exalted level in the Divine Hierarchy.

In the case we are considering—the founding of
the Fourth Root Race—it was one of the Adepts
from Venus who undertook the duties of the Manu.
Naturally he belonged to a very high order, for it
must be understood that the Beings who came from
the Venus system as rulers and teachers of our infant
humanity did *not* all stand at the same level. It is this
circumstance which furnishes a reason for the remarkable fact that may, in conclusion, be stated—
namely, that there existed in Lemuria a Lodge of Initiation.

A Lodge of Initiation

Naturally it was not for the benefit of the Lemurian
race that the Lodge was founded. Such of them as
were sufficiently advanced were, it is true, taught by

the Adept Gurus, but the instruction they required was limited to the explanation of a few physical phenomena, such as the fact that the earth moves round the sun, or to the explanation of the different appearance which physical objects assumed for them when subjected alternately to their physical sight and their astral vision.

It was, of course, for the sake of those who, while endowed with the stupendous powers of transferring their consciousness from the planet Venus to this our earth, and of providing for their use and their work while here appropriate vehicles in which to function, were yet pursuing the course of their own evolution.* For their sake it was—for the sake of those who, having entered the Path, had only reached the lower grades, that this Lodge of Initiation was founded.

Though, as we know, the goal of normal evolution is greater and more glorious than can, from our present standpoint, be well imagined, it is by no means synonymous with that expansion of consciousness which, combined with and alone made possible by, the purification and ennoblement of character, constitute the heights to which the Pathway of Initiation leads.

The investigation into what constitutes this purification and ennoblement of character, and the endeavour to realise what that expansion of con-

---

*The heights reached by them will find their parallel when our humanity will, countless aeons hence, have reached the Sixth Round of our chain of worlds, and the same transcendent powers will be the possession of ordinary mankind in those far-off ages.

sciousness really means are subjects which have been written of elsewhere.

Suffice it now to point out that the founding of a Lodge of Initiation for the sake of Beings who came from another scheme of evolution is an indication of the unity of object and of aim in the government and the guidance of *all* the schemes of evolution brought into existence by our Solar Logos. Apart from the normal course in our own scheme, there is, we know, a Path by which He may be directly reached, which every son of man in his progress through the ages is privileged to hear of, and to tread, if he so chooses. We find that this was so in the Venus scheme also, and we may presume it is or will be so in all the schemes which form part of our Solar system. This Path is the Path of Initiation, and the end to which leads is the same for all, and that end is Union with God.

Index

QUEST BOOKS
are published by
The Theosophical Society in America,
Wheaton, Illinois 60189-0270,
a branch of a world organization
dedicated to the promotion of the unity of
humanity and the encouragement of the study of
religion, philosophy, and science, to the end that
we may better understand ourselves and our place in
the universe. The Society stands for complete
freedom of individual search and belief.
In the Classics Series well-known
theosophical works are made
available in popular editions.
For more information
write or call.

1-708-668-1571